£2·95

Documents and Debates
General Editor: John Wroughton M.A., F.R.Hist.S

Twentieth-Century Britain

Richard Brown
Houghton Regis Upper School, Bedfordshire

Christopher Daniels
Royal Latin School, Buckingham
Schoolteacher Fellow Commoner,
Sidney Sussex College, Cambridge 1982

MACMILLAN

IN MEMORIAM MERVYN JOHN BROWN 1919–81
who taught me about Twentieth Century Britain

TO DEBBIE, KATE, DENISE, CATHY AND KATIE:
HISTORIANS

First published 1982
Reprinted 1984, 1985

Published by
MACMILLAN EDUCATION LTD
Houndmills, Basingstoke, Hampshire RG21 2XS
and London
Companies and representatives
throughout the world

Printed in Hong Kong

British Library Cataloguing in Publication Data

Twentieth century Britain. – (Documents and
    debates)
    1. Great Britain – History – 20th century
    I. Brown, Richard   II. Daniels, Christopher
    III. Series
    941.082   DA566

ISBN 0-333-31285-6

Contents

Acknowledgements

The author and publishers wish to thank the following who have kindly given permission for the use of copyright material:

Associated Book Publishers for extracts from *The Conservative Party From Peel to Churchill* by R Blake, and *British Government 1914–1953* by G le May, published by Eyre Methuen Ltd;

The Bodley Head for extracts from *The British Experience 1945–75* by Peter Calvocoressi (1978);

The British Broadcasting Corporation and Nicholas Pronay for extracts from *Illusions of Reality: Men of the Hour*, a television documentary written by Nicholas Pronay and produced by Howard Smith;

Jonathan Cape Ltd for extracts from *The Slump: Society and Politics during the Depression* by John Stevenson and Chris Cook (1977);

Chatto and Windus Ltd on behalf of the Owen Estate for the poem 'Anthem for Doomed Youth' from *The Collected Poems of Wilfred Owen*, edited by C Day Lewis;

The Controller of Her Majesty's Stationery Office for extracts from *Government of Ireland Act 1920*, *Social Insurance and Allied Services Cnd 6404* and Hansard Vol. 82;

The Comptroller of Her Majesty's Stationery Office, The Deputy Keeper of the Records of Northern Ireland and Captain Peter Montgomery for a letter from Hugh de F. Montgomery of the Ulster Unionist Council to his son 22.6.1916 in the Montgomery papers, ref. P.R.O.N.I. ref. D627/429/44;

Constable & Co. Ltd for extracts from *No End of a Lesson* by Anthony Nutting (1967);

William Collins & Co. Ltd for an extract from *The Downfall of the Liberal Party* by Trevor Wilson (1968);

Curtis Brown Academic Ltd on behalf of William McElwee for extracts from *Britain's Locust Years 1918–1940*, copyright © William McElwee 1962;

Andre Deutsch Ltd for an extract from *The Affluent Society* by J K Galbraith (1958);

Emberdove Ltd and the Trustees of the Broadlands Archives for extracts from an address by Viscount Mountbatten of Burma to the Indian Constituent Assembly at New Delhi, 15 August 1947;

John Farquharson Ltd on behalf of R V Jones for an extract from *Most Secret War* published by Hamish Hamilton Ltd and Coronet Books;

Fontana Paperbacks for an extract and tables from *Women at War 1914–1918* by Arthur Marwick (1977), an extract from *Britain and the Second World War* by H Pelling (1970), and an extract from *Britain and the World Economy 1919–70* by L J Williams (1971);

Victor Gollancz Ltd for extracts from *Testament of Youth* by Vera Brittain (1933);

Hamish Hamilton Ltd for extracts from *Public and Private* by Humphrey Trevelyan (1980) and *A Man of the Times* by Iverach McDonald (1976);

A M Heath & Co. Ltd on behalf of Mrs Sonia Brownwell Orwell and the Estate of the late George Orwell, for an extract from *The Road to Wigan Pier* (1937), published by Martin Secker & Warburg;

William Heinemann Ltd for an extract from *English Journey* by J B Priestley;

David Higham Associates Ltd on behalf of Philip Guedalla for an extract from *Mr Churchill, A Portrait* (1941);

The International Economic Association for an extract from *The Economic Consequences of the Peace* by J M Keynes (1919);

Lord Lothian, The Twelfth Marquess of Lothian, for an extract from a letter from the Eleventh Marquess of Lothian to Lloyd George;

The London School of Economics and Political Science for extracts from *Beatrice Webb, Diaries 1912–1924*, edited by Margaret Cole (1952);

Longman Group Ltd for extracts from *Rise of the Labour Party 1880–1945* by P Adelman (1972);

The New American Library Inc. for extracts from *The Roots of Appeasement* by Martin Gilbert, copyright © 1966;

Orient Longman Ltd for extracts from *Transfer of Power in India* by V P Menon (1957);

Oxford University Press for an extract from *English History 1914–1945* by A J P Taylor (1965) and for an extract, letter by Wilfred Owen reprinted in *Collected Letters* edited by Harold Owen and John Bell (1967);

Oxford University Press Inc. New York, for an extract from *Chemistry Decoded* by Leonard W Fine, copyright © 1976;

The Past and Present Society, Corpus Christi College, Oxford, for extracts from an article by Dr R McKibbin in *Past and Present: a Journal of Historical Studies* No. 68 August 1975;

A D Peters & Co. Ltd on behalf of Arthur Marwick for an extract from *Britain in the Century of Total War*, published by The Bodley Head (1968), and on behalf of Robert Skidelsky for an extract from *Politicians and the Slump: the Labour Government of 1929–31*;

Penguin Books Ltd for extracts from *Divided Ulster* by Liam de Paor (Penguin Special 1970) Copyright © Liam de Paor 1970, 1971; *The Stagnant Society* by Michael Shanks (Pelican Books Revised Edition 1972) Copyright © Michael Shanks 1961, 1972; 'The Statesman' by A J P Taylor from *Churchill: Four Faces and the Man* by A J P Taylor et al (Allen Lane/The Penguin Press 1969) Copyright © A J P Taylor 1968, and *Post-War Britain: A Political History* by Alan Sked and Chris Cook (Pelican Books 1979) Copyright © Alan Sked and Chris Cook 1979;

Dr A L Rowse for an extract from *All Souls and Appeasement* (1961);

Weidenfeld & Nicolson Ltd for extracts from *The Scope of Happiness* by V L Pandit (1979) and *Churchill: A Study in Failure 1900–1939* by R R James (1970).

Every effort has been made to trace all the copyright holders but if any have been inadvertently overlooked the publishers will be pleased to make the necessary arrangement at the first opportunity.

Cover photograph: 'Let us Go Forward Together' (detail) Second World War Poster, Courtesy of Trustees of the Imperial War Museum.

The authors wish to extend particular thanks to the following for assistance given in the preparation of this book: Nicholas Pronay of Leeds University, Edward Grimsdale of the Royal Latin School, Buckingham, John Shoard and John Stevenson; thanks are also due to the Bodleian Library, Oxford, to Buckingham Public Library and to the Archives Départmentalles d'Ille-et-Vilaine, Rennes.

From Armageddon to the New Jerusalem?
British History from 1918 to 1964

Historians tend to look at the history of Britain since 1890 in terms of decades. The 'Naughty Nineties' were followed by the Edwardian era; *the* War was followed by the frivolous twenties; and then came the depressed thirties, the austere forties, the affluent fifties, the illusory sixties and the inflationary seventies. This periodisation is both useful and misleading. Its value lies in the identification by historians of the underlying trends of a particular decade. It can also be misleading since these stereotypes have given rise to the development of a mythology of change into which events are sometimes compelled to fit.

The twentieth century is undeniably a period of fast, many would claim revolutionary, change. This applies to Britain as much as to the rest of the world. Yet for Britain this change is founded upon a very weak base. In 1918 Britain could claim, with real conviction, that she was one of the peacemakers of the world. By 1945 this claim was a mere chimera. Yet Britain remained throughout much of this period a country whose self-image was basically a mirage. Suez ended this illusion. If economic strength is the basis of political strength and standing, then Britain's decline – if that is the best way to describe it – began in the 1870s. Britain's economic supremacy in the early and mid-nineteenth century was based upon a combination of global exports and free trade. From 1870 both of these were increasingly challenged: the first through the development of foreign competitors like Germany and the USA, and the second through being maintained long after it had real economic benefits.

In particular, the war of 1914–18 sounded the death knell of the increasingly obsolete British economy, in its early industrial sense. Britain's position was based largely on her staple industries – textiles, iron and steel, shipbuilding and coal – and these proved increasingly uncompetitive in the inter-war period. The economic effects of war were detrimental to the British economy: war – especially 'total war' – placed a burden on British industry which it was unable to bear in the long term. The development of new, consumer-based industries certainly relieved the economic pressures but it only delayed a long-term process of decline. Despite this, the industrial base with its problems of adjustment and distribution was sufficient to allow for an absolute rise in output and rising living standards. The chapters on the social and economic effects of war and on the politics of the post-1945 era illustrate the character of this problem. War led to social reform in both 1918 and 1945, the first largely unsuccessful because of financial constraints, the second only successful because it was accepted by the major political parties and was viewed as an alternative to complete social transformation. The illusion of economic prosperity was made clear in the late 1950s when successive Conservative governments failed to solve the basic problems of the economy; an economic deluge is often preceded by a period of illusory affluence.

In 1918 British politics was based upon the relationship between Liberal and Conservative parties. They were, in many ways, sides of the same coin. They accepted both the logic of consensus politics and the benefits of a capitalist society. By 1924 this had been replaced by governments of Labour and Conservative parties. The Liberals found themselves 'between the Devil and the deep blue sea'. Yet even the emergence of a working-class party did not alter the basis of politics. Consensus and Capitalism remained the basis of political life. Both Baldwin and Ramsay Macdonald accepted the logic of this situation. The General Strike of 1926 demonstrated the unwillingness of even radical trade unionists to push the system too far. The formation of the National Government in 1931 showed the extent to which the Labour leadership accepted the conservative economic philosophy.

The post-war period up to 1964 saw this consensual basis of politics continue. Both parties, Conservative and Labour, accepted the need for a Welfare State, even though they may have differed over the better solution to the problem. The Conservatives accepted the Keynesian ideas of a 'mixed economy' and 'full employment' as quickly as did the Labour Party, once the bankruptcy of the old classical view of economics was made clear in the 1930s. The hegemony of the Conservatives in the inter-war period has been replaced by the alternation of Conservative and Labour since 1945. Only in the late 1950s did consensus come into question and its illusory nature become clear. The basis of British politics was now questioned and found wanting. The General Elections of 1964 and 1966 brought people into Parliament willing to question its almost sanctified character.

Lloyd George was perhaps the dominant figure at the Versailles conference in 1919. Britain possessed an empire which covered large parts of the world and which had played an important part in the victory. Yet she found great difficulty in resolving divergent views on the question of Ireland. Time has shown that the settlement which Lloyd George introduced between 1920 and 1922 was unsound, based as it was upon the partition of an island – always a dangerous answer. The 1960s have made it clear that this solution was based on illusions.

Appeasement in the 1930s falls into the same category. The illusion that concession to Hitler was the answer to his aggressive tendencies was rightly criticised by Churchill and others at the time. The alternative to appeasement, however, was war, which was politically dangerous since voters remembered the First World War with great fear. The movement from Empire to Commonwealth was one area where Britain acted in accord with the wishes of those areas colonised. The events of 1931, the Second World War and the incipient nationalism of the colonies all led to the 'winds of change' emerging. The case of India shows how well decolonisation could be handled, as well as the often violent aftermath of the process, while Suez shows imperialism gone mad.

Britain in 1964 was therefore a very different place from Britain in 1918: no longer pre-eminent though some politicians still thought she was. The logic of the British political system was being brought into question and the illusory nature of British power made clear. Britain may be unwilling to leave the global stage, but she is now very much like an actor without a clear role to play.

'History is an Argument without End' (Pieter Geyl)

Gordon Leff once argued that:

it is precisely the dynamic, relative character of history, its preoccupation with the specific and the concrete, its lack of regularity, that makes it indispensable to all social and human understanding; and . . . the rejection of the old notion of historical destiny for that of the future as open gives history a greater importance now, when so much more depends upon our conscious choices, than in the past.

What then is the historian's task? G. R. Elton wrote that it is:

to discover, reconstruct and explain what has happened in the past from such survivals of the past as are found in the present. The pervasive problems facing him are two: the extant evidence is always incomplete and usually highly ambiguous, and in trying to understand and explain that evidence he inescapably introduces the (possibly distorting) subjectivity of his own mind.

The sources for the twentieth century are far wider than for any previous period, but some of these sources are, alas, quite inaccessible. The width extends to newsreels, films and photographs (some of which show that the camera can be made to lie) and there is also the developing field of 'oral history' where people who experienced many of the events in this book are interviewed. The historical examination of newsreel archives is a fascinating topic, and Nicholas Pronay's articles in *History* (October 1971; February 1972) are illuminating on the manipulation of cinema audiences between the wars by the five main newsreel companies. Unfortunately, cost and technical difficulties made it impossible to include a video-cassette with a newsreel compilation to extend the range of the book, but suggestions are made in chapter VII on how to investigate this subject. The advent of the telephone has lessened the flow of letters common to earlier periods but the main problems for the contemporary historian are the wealth of the material and the secrecy that surrounds some of it. Many government documents are 'frozen' for thirty years under the Public Records Act, 1967, and there is a reluctance to disclose controversial evidence during the lifetime of those involved; this affects, for example, the Sèvres conference, 1956.

Are we too close to the events of the present century to view them objectively? The events of the Second World War have largely been fitted into the framework adopted by Winston Churchill in his six-volume history (cf. chapter V of the present book), but A. J. P. Taylor has argued recently that the German invasion of Russia in June 1941 was the real starting point, and that the war between Britain and Germany – hardly a world war – had reached a stalemate by 1941. Is this an example of the importance of 'distance'?

How does the historian avoid the danger of allowing the terms of his inquiry to dictate what he discovers, what J. H. Hexter has referred to as 'source-mining'? Elton's answer is that 'the material must be evaluated in its own terms and in relation to what surrounds it.' (This is the importance of setting a document in its historical context.) And as Martin Gilbert said, 'Evidence is something you play with as a kitten plays with a ball of wool.' Readers should consider the following questions while using this book: Why have the authors chosen these ten subjects for inclusion? On what grounds have the documents within them been selected? What are the authors' unstated assumptions about Britain in this century? Why are the sources almost exclusively written or printed? To what extent do the questions direct the debate of which the sources are a part? Have the documents been unfairly edited ('I am a severe critic of the three dot brigade. One has constantly to make the decision where to end the quotation, but I have formed a rule: never take something out of the middle of a sentence': Martin Gilbert)? Do the documents reveal what Arthur Marwick described as 'witting testimony' (information which the document compiler intended to convey) and 'unwitting testimony' (assumptions underlying the document)?

One of the aims of using documents is to breathe life into the study of the past. When A. J. P. Taylor wrote his book *The Origins of the Second World War* (cf. *Twentieth Century Europe*, chapter VIII) he was accused of turning the past into a game in which traditional interpretations are inverted; but history is not a game but life itself, where problems were taken very seriously by contemporaries. Many of the themes in this book like Ireland, India, the Middle East, the Welfare State or the role of Britain in world affairs are highly topical, and some of the personalities of twentieth-century Britain are more than just names: men like Churchill, Attlee and Macmillan.

But the documents selected for this book are not merely illustrative; using evidence encourages the forming of opinions which, if historically valid, 'become subsumed into an ever growing agglomerate of interpretation.' (G. R. Elton) The debates sections are not arid disputations solely for specialists in a particular field; they are at the heart of the study of history because there are no closed issues and no 'authorities' in history. New knowledge and new thought, the latter often reflecting the age in which it takes place, are always visible in the study of history, and the only weight is the quality of the argument. This is the historical dialectic: the debate between the historian and his evidence, and between historians, whether 'teacher' or 'student'. Recreating the past requires not merely a careful, systematic, questioning approach to sources but a disciplined use of the imagination. Evidence is not fitted into a pattern like pieces of a jigsaw but reacts with the intellect to produce an account of what happened and why. The disputants advance various hypothetical interpretations which, hopefully, lead to clearer understanding.

Several of these documents illustrate the importance of 'the unexpected, the unforeseen, the contingent, the accidental and the unknowable.' (G. R. Elton) In one of the books used in chapter V, R. R. James explains this in relation to the Chanak incident of 1922:

> In any crisis of this nature the historian, however well equipped with information, is at a disadvantage. Any crisis generates its own momentum and its own personality. The stress of events; fragmentary information; the characters of individual ministers; physical tiredness; sheer chance: all these play their part, and contribute to the character and development of the crisis to an extent of which even the participants are often unaware. And thus it is that follies are committed and a sense of proportion lost for reasons which are impossible to specify with any exactness. Thus, however complete the documentation may be, the true causes are usually absent.

This is where history can be confusing, in that at one level there is popular mythology of events (e.g. Dunkirk, 1940) and at another, as Jacob Burckhardt wrote, history 'is on every occasion the record of what one age finds worthy of note in another.' Here is Leff on the subject:

> For the human studies there is an element of myth inherent in human thinking and conduct. It represents man's response to his world, and runs in a spectrum from the image that we have of ourselves to that which we have of the cosmos.
> We inherit a body of beliefs and judgments which make up a kind of collective historical unconscious. It is one of the most formative elements in our lives. For not only does it colour our attitudes to the world but it produces a time-lag in our thinking which can persist over centuries. It is to be seen in conventions, practices, techniques, habits, institutions, which prevail within a society at any given time, and are often so far removed from their origins that they have become either mere ritual or a fetter upon new developments, especially in times of rapid change, as in our society today [1969]. But at the very least we are always one generation behind events, because each generation grows up under the influence of the ideas and experiences of the previous generation. It is a historical truism that the subalterns in the Flanders trenches from 1914 to 1918 were the generals who were confounded by Blitzkrieg in 1940, and that our rulers, brought up to believe in an empire on which the sun never set, can even now hardly bring themselves to preside over its final dissolution. The process is ineluctable. It gives rise at one level to the clash between generations: the laments about youth and our loss of values today can be matched almost word for word from any past epoch. But it also leads to the divergences within generations and society itself. . . .
> . . . Men are what they are, and history is what it is, in virtue of the beliefs which they hold and on which they act. Because they are contingent, as diverse as the possible outcomes and individuals who can realise them, history is indispensable to understanding what is indispensable to men.

These are valuable discussion points during work on documents and debates; working at them the student historian, like one of C. P. Snow's characters in *The Masters*, can appreciate the complexities of human life at various levels:

For Brown loved his friends, and knew they were only men. Since they were only men, they could be treacherous – and then next time loyal beyond belief. One took them as they were . . . .

Further Reading

E. H. Carr, *What is History?* (Macmillan, 1961)
G. R. Elton, *The Practice of History* (Collins/Fontana 1969)
G. Kitson Clark, *The Critical Historian* (Heinemann, 1967)
G. Leff, *History and Social Theory* (The Merlin Press, 1969)
A. Marwick, *The Nature of History* (Macmillan, 1970)
Open University, *Introduction to History* (A101 Arts Foundation Course Units 3–5, 1977)
J. H. Plumb, *The Death of the Past* (Macmillan, 1969)

I Britain and the Impact of Total War

Introduction

The memories of the two world wars still linger in the 1980s, seventy years after the outbreak of the first, and forty since the close of the second. The survival of Remembrance Day, a reminder and an echo of the jubilant Armistice Day portrayed by Vera Brittain, keeps alive the horror, squalor and inhumanity of both wars while equally extolling the dignity, bravery and fortitude of those who kept this country free in its struggle to prevent domination of Europe by one great power. During the second of these wars the British lost an empire, yet inaugurated – with the publication of the Beveridge Report in 1942 – a valuable and far-reaching scheme of comprehensive social welfare. The debate popularised by Arthur Marwick on the extent to which war accelerated or caused social change is illustrated in this section with reference to medicine, science (in particular, radio waves and atomic energy) and the role of women in society. This view has not gone unchallenged as the contribution by Henry Pelling shows.

The First World War was a deep shock to all who experienced it, and the war poets – like Wilfred Owen – produced brilliant, often pathetic or vituperative but always compelling, pieces of literature on the trench warfare of the Western Front. The experience scarred many deeply, like Vera Brittain who lost her closest friends and her brother in this conflict, and the traumatic effects were clearly visible on many of the inter-war politicians like Chamberlain and Eden, the latter of whom had once sorted through a heap of dead bodies to identify them.

Despite the involvement of the 'common man' in these wars – especially civilians in the Second World War – many of the accounts remain those of educated people. The Imperial War Museum in London has developed an oral history section for personal memoirs of the wars, and these can be consulted. As in other sections of this book, the use of film as a major source is vital, and access to good examples or compilations is not difficult, nor should drama be discounted, as the excellent BBC Television version of *Testament of Youth* illustrated in the late 1970s.

Further Reading

A. Calder, *The People's War, Britain 1939–45* (Jonathan Cape, 1969), a very detailed and informative study of the effects of total war on

Britain, which deserves to be read in full for its descriptive writing rather than for its arguments.

H. Fyfe, *Britain's War-Time Revolution* (Gollancz, 1944), a left-wing, controversial, and often amusing viewpoint of the social effects of the war, first serialised in *Reynold's News*.

R. V. Jones, *Most Secret War* (Hamish Hamilton, 1978), without doubt the best account of scientific intelligence in the Second World War; well written with many pungent comments on then and now.

L. Macdonald, *They Called It Passchendaele* (Michael Joseph, 1978), largely based on first-hand interviews with survivors of the Ypres salient, this is a poignant and informative account.

A. Marwick, *The Deluge: British Society and the First World War* (Bodley Head, 1965), a stimulating discussion of the social and economic impact of the First World War.

A. Marwick, *War and Social Change in the Twentieth Century* (Macmillan, 1974), Marwick's third and perhaps least successful venture on his thesis of war and social change; this one is a comparative study of the major powers.

Open University third level Arts course *War and Society*, a Marwick-dominated multi-disciplinary course, whose units on the twentieth century (including radio and television programmes) offer a great deal of material as evidence for discussion.

A. S. Milward, *The Economic Effects of the Two World Wars on Britain* (Macmillan, 1970), an outline of the main arguments on war, social change and the economy, with examples from Britain set in a wide context. Milward supports the 'Marwick thesis' but does not think the changes were very great.

D. Winter, *Death's Men* (Allen Lane, 1978), an introduction to the nature of warfare on the Western Front which looks at men as well as *matériel*.

1   War and Social Change

[My basic contention] is that two wars have played a substantial, though unequal, part in furthering social change in twentieth-century Britain. . . .

War . . . is a matter of loss and gain: loss of life and limb and capital;
5   gain of territory, indemnities or trade concessions. War is the supreme challenge to, and test of, a country's military institutions, and, in a war of any size, a challenge to its social, political and economic institutions as well. War needs someone to do the fighting, and someone to furnish the weapons and food: those who participate in the war effort have to be
10 rewarded. . . . War is one of the most intense emotional experiences (comparable only with the great revolutions in history) in which human beings as members of a community can be involved. . . .

In passing judgement upon the use made by Britain of the potential of science the war raised two questions: was existing scientific knowledge

15 being fully exploited, and were sufficient resources being devoted
towards extending existing scientific knowledge? . . .

   The harvest was most golden in the field of nutrition, where intensive
research made it possible to maintain a high dietary level for the whole
population despite the worst scarcities of food, and in the control of
20 infectious disease. . . . The defects in pre-war lower-class diets were well
known, but it was only after the outbreak of war that the M[edical]
R[esearch] C[ouncil] was able successfully to advocate the provision of
extra milk, cod-liver oil . . . and the addition of vitamins D and A
to . . . margarine, and of calcium to bread. Immunization with tetanus
25 toxoid was known before the war, but its use was effectively proved
during the war. Similarly the Swiss discovery of D.D.T. was first used on
a large scale against louse-borne typhus. . . . The most celebrated
example . . . was . . . [the] development of Sir Alexander Fleming's
neglected discovery of penicillin. But here the challenge of war merged
30 with its destructive influence. While fighting for survival Britain simply
could not afford the resources to exploit to the full the pioneer work of
her own scientists: in 1941 . . . Florey and his assistant Dr Heatley went
to the United States, where penicillin was produced on a massive scale.
The gains to mankind were enormous, but not least among the
35 beneficiaries was the American pharmaceuticals industry. . . . Advances
were also made in the development of blood transfusion services, skin
grafting, plastic surgery, anaesthesia and the treatment of 'traumatic
shock' (the 'shell-shock' of the former war). . . .

   Mr A. J. P. Taylor concluded his *English History 1914–45* by remarking
40 that 'in the Second World War the British people came of age'. Apart
from the specific context in which he used the phrase, this was true also in
the sense that at the end of the war the majority had a clearer idea than
ever before of what it was they expected of a modern civilized industrial
society: decent living standards, income and health security, a taste of the
45 modest luxuries of life: once the idea was defined it became in itself an
agent of further change. In addition to this the war hastened the scientific,
technological and economic processes which . . . were trans-
forming . . . society. The 'wireless' had become a national property
during the war . . . ; mass television was on the way. A National Health
50 Service with new drugs at its disposal would be twice as effective in
stamping out the diseases that had been a special affliction of the lower
classes. . . .

   A. Marwick, *Britain in the Century of Total War*, Bodley Head
   1968 [Penguin edn 1970], pp. 12–13, 284–6, 322–3

Questions

a   Identify Marwick's four basic themes on the effects of war.
b   What advances were made during the Second World War in (a)
    dietary nutrition; (b) medicine? Were these new discoveries or an
    acceleration of the process between discovery and production?
c   How does Marwick extend the quotation from A. J. P. Taylor (lines
    39–40)?

* *d* What are the connections between the social changes of 1942–51 and Marwick's views on the impact of war (cf. chapter VIII)?

* *e* Is the theme of war and social change applicable only to the 'total wars' of the twentieth century?

2 Women at War

The imposition of universal conscription was an event of central importance in the social history of the war: it began the second and definitive growth in women's employment and determined that the changes involved should go far beyond a limited expansion and
5 upgrading of industrial labour, given additional piquancy by the entry for the first time into hard physical work of a few adventurous members of the upper classes. Just two weeks after the passing of the Act, the Government launched its first national drive to fill the places vacated or about to be vacated by men. . . .
10 In July 1914 there had been 212,000 women employed in the various metal and engineering industries that were to become the ones most directly connected with war production. The figure for July 1915, 256,000, shows only a relatively small increase; but [by next July it was] 520,000 . . . by July 1917 . . . the figure was 819,000. . . .
15 In industry as a whole the total employment of women and girls over 10 had increased between 1914 and 1918 by about 800,000. . . .
By February 1917 the total number of bus conductresses had jumped up . . . to around two and a half thousand. . . . It is transport that shows the biggest proportionate increase in women's employment – from
20 18,000 in 1914 to 117,000 in 1918. After transport the biggest proportional increases were in clerical, commercial, administrative and educational activities. In banking and finance there was a fantastic rate of growth – from a mere 9,500 . . . in 1914 to 63,700 in 1917. . . . It is in these arid statistics that we encounter a central phenomenon in the
25 sociology of women's employment in the twentieth century, the rise of the business girl. . . . The war . . . in creating simultaneously a proliferation of Government Committees and departments and a shortage of men, brought a sudden and irreversible advance in the economic and social power of a category of women employees. . . .
30 Women worked as lamplighters and as window cleaners. They also did very heavy work in gasworks and foundries, carrying bags of coke and working among the furnaces. . . . One of the simple remedies used when the women succumbed to the arduous conditions . . .[is remembered]: 'Many is the time the girls would be affected by the gas, the remedy being
35 to walk them up and down in the fresh air, and then drink a bottle of Guinness.'
Despite repeated . . . government-initiated attempts to recruit women workers for the land, these had not been conspicuously successful. In July 1915 there were about 20,000 less permanent female
40 workers on the land than in July 1914 – as in the case of domestic service the war had provided a blessed release. . . .

Table 1
Some Broad Census Data England and Wales Only

	Total Population	Total females	Over 10 years	Total females occupied	married	widowed	Females per 1,000 males	Females per 1,000 males in age group 20–45
1901	32,527,843	16,799,230	13,189,585	4,171,751	917,509		1,068	1,068
1911	36,070,492	18,624,884	14,357,113	4,830,734	680,191	411,011	1,068	1,095
			Over 12 years					
1921	37,886,699	19,811,460	15,699,805	5,065,332	693,034	425,981	1,096	1,172
			Over 14 years					
1931	39,952,377	20,819,367	16,419,894	5,606,043	896,702	389,187	1,088	

Table 2
Women in Munitions (Metal and Chemical Trades) – Great Britain and Ireland
Private Factories and Government Factories

☐ Private   ▨ Government

July 1914: Total 212,000 / Private 210,000
Conscription for men, Jan. and May 1915
Ministry of Munitions May 1915
July 1915: 256,000 / 253,000
July 1916
July 1917: 819,000 / 616,000
November 1918: 947,000 / 700,000
July 1920: 379,000 / 373,000

Table 3
Other Occupations Great Britain and Ireland

	1914	1918
Transport	18 200	117 200
Municipal Tramways	1 200	18 800
Private	200	5 800
Buses	300	4 300
Railways	12 000	65 000
Commerce	505 200	934 500
Banking	1 500	37 600
Insurance	7 000	32 300
Agriculture	190 000	228 000
National and Local Government (including education)	262 200	460 200
Hotels, Public Houses, Theatres etc.	181 000	220 000
Industry	2 178 600	2 970 600
Textile trades	863 000	818 000
Clothing trades	612 000	556 000
Domestic Service	1 658 000	1 250 000
On own account or as Employers	430 000	470 000
Professional, home workers etc. (including nurses, secretaries and typists)	542 000	652 500
Altogether in occupations	5 966 000	7 311 000
Not in occupations but over 10	12 946 000	12 496 000
Under 10	4 809 000	4 731 000
Total females	23 721 000	24 538 000

To say that the war brought votes for women is to make a very crude generalization, yet one which contains essential truth. . . . One must see the question of women's rights not in isolation, but as part of a wider context of social relationships and political change. . . . The political advance of women in 1914 was still blocked by two great fortresses of prejudice: the vigorous hostility of men, and the often fearful reluctance . . . of many women . . . . [The war] brought a new confidence to women, dissipated apathy, silenced the female anti-suffragists. . . . Undoubtedly the replacement of militant . . . activity by frantic patriotic endeavour played its part as well.

More than this, the war generated a tremendous mood favourable to change and democratic innovations . . . . Whatever might or might not have happened had there been no war, only the war could have provided the concentrated experience which both gave to women a new confidence in themselves, and showed up the absurdities of the many preconceptions about what they were capable of . . . . E. S. Montague, Lloyd George's successor as Minister of Munitions, . . . [said] on 15 August 1916 . . . 'Women of every station . . . have proved themselves

60   able to undertake work that before the war was regarded as solely the
      province of men. . . . Where . . . is the man now who would deny to
      women the civil rights which she has earned by her hard work?'
              A. Marwick, *Women at War 1914—1918*, Croom Helm, 1977, pp.
          73—4, 78—9, 157—8, 166

Questions

a   What was the importance to women's employment of the introduc-
    tion of conscription in 1916?

b   Using the information in the text and the statistical tables, comment
    on the occupations taken up or rejected by women.

c   'The great searchlight of war showed things in their true light, and
    they gave us enfranchisement with open hands.' (Millicent Garrett
    Fawcett, January 1918) What reasons does Marwick give which
    favour this comment?

* d   To what extent does the historian have to use caution in handling this
       material in view of Marwick's known views on war and social change
       (cf. document 1)?

* e   Investigate the extent to which the Second World War altered this
       picture of the opportunities – social and political – for women.
       How has the situation changed between 1945 and the present day?

3   Testament of Youth

When the sound of victorious guns burst over London at 11 a.m. on
November 11th, 1918, the men and women who looked incredulously
into each other's faces did not cry jubilantly: 'We've won the War!' They
only said: 'The War is over.'

5   From Millbank I heard the maroons crash with terrifying clearness,
and, like a sleeper who is determined to go on dreaming after being told
to wake up, I went on automatically washing the dressing bowls in the
annex outside my hut. Deeply buried beneath my consciousness there
stirred the vague memory of a letter that I had written to Roland in those
10   legendary days when I was still at Oxford, and could spend my Sundays
in thinking of him while the organ echoed grandly through New College
Chapel. It had been a warm May evening, when all the city was sweet
with the scent of wallflowers and lilac, and I had walked back to Micklem
Hall after hearing an Occasional Oratorio by Handel, which described
15   the mustering of troops for battle, the lament for the fallen and the
triumphant return of the victors. . . .

     But on Armistice Day not even a lonely survivor drowning in black
waves of memory could be left alone with her thoughts. A moment after
the guns had subsided into sudden, palpitating silence, the other V.A.D.
20   from my ward dashed excitedly into the annex.

     'Brittain! Brittain! Did you hear the maroons? It's over — it's all over!
Do let's come out and see what's happening!' . . .

I followed her into the road. As I stood there, stupidly rigid . . . I saw a
taxicab turn swiftly in from the Embankment towards the hospital. The
25 next moment there was a cry . . . for in rounding the corner the taxi had
knocked down a small elderly woman. . . .

As I hurried to her side I realised that she was all but dead . . . but on
the tiny chalk-white face an expression of shocked surprise still
lingered. . . . Had she been thinking . . . of her sons at the front, now
30 safe? . . .

Late that evening . . . a group of elated V.A.D.s . . . prevailed upon
me to join them. Outside the Admiralty a crazy group of convalescent
Tommies were collecting specimens of different uniforms and bundling
their wearers into flag-strewn taxis. . . . Wherever we went a burst of
35 enthusiastic cheering greeted our Red Cross uniform, and complete
strangers adorned with wound stripes rushed up and shook me warmly
by the hand. . . .

I detached myself from the others and walked slowly up Whitehall,
with my heart sinking in a sudden cold dismay. Already this was a
40 different world from the one that I had known during four life-long
years, a world in which people would be light-hearted and forgetful, in
which themselves and their careers and their amusements would blot out
political ideals and great national issues. And in that brightly lit, alien
world I should have no part. All those with whom I had really been
45 intimate were gone; not one remained to share with me the heights and
the depths of my memories. As the years went by and youth departed and
remembrance grew dim, a deeper and ever deeper darkness would cover
the young men who were once my contemporaries.

For the first time I realised, with all that full realisation meant, how
50 completely everything that had hitherto made up my life had vanished
with Edward and Roland, with Victor and Geoffrey. The War was over;
a new age was beginning; but the dead were dead and would never
return.

V. Brittain, *Testament of Youth*, Gollancz, 1933 [Virago-Fontana
edn 1979], pp. 460–63

Questions

a   What war service was Vera Brittain occupied in at this time? What is
the evidence for this?
b   What is reflected in the difference between 'We've won the War!' and
'The War is over.' (lines 3–4)?
c   Why did Vera not take as exuberant a part in the festivities in London
as many others?
d   'Already this was a different world from the one that I had known
during four life-long years' (lines 39–41). Why did Vera think this?
* e   If one of the aims of the study of history is to achieve understanding of
the past and of the views of people in the past, how effective is this
remembrance of the end of the First World War?

* f What link is there between the viewpoint of this document and the outlook of many British people and politicians in the inter-war period?

4 The Agony of War

I have not been at the front.

I have been in front of it.

I held an advanced post, that is, a 'dug-out' in the middle of No Man's Land.

5   We had a march of 3 miles over shelled road then nearly 3 along a flooded trench. After that we came to where the trenches had been blown flat out and had to go over the top. It was of course dark, too dark, and the ground was not mud, not sloppy mud, but an octopus of sucking clay, 3, 4, and 5 feet deep, relieved only by craters full of water. Men have been
10   known to drown in them. Many stuck in the mud and only got on by leaving their waders, equipment, and in some cases their clothes.

High explosives were dropping all around us, and machine guns spluttered every few minutes. But it was so dark that even the German flares did not reveal us.

15   Three quarters dead, I mean each of us ¾ dead, we reached the dug-out, and relieved the wretches therein. I then had to go forth and find another dug-out for a still more advanced post where I had left 18 bombers. I was responsible for other posts on the left but there was a junior officer in charge.

20   My dug-out held 25 men tight packed. Water filled in to a depth of 1 or 2 feet, leaving say 4 feet of air.

One entrance had been blown in and blocked.

So far, the other remained.

The Germans knew we were staying there and decided we shouldn't.

25   Those fifty hours were the agony of my happy life.

Every ten minutes on Sunday afternoon seemed an hour.

I nearly broke down and let myself drown in the water that was now slowly rising over my knees.

Towards 6 o'clock, when, I suppose, you would be going to church,
30   the shelling grew less intense and less accurate: so that I was mercifully helped to do my duty and crawl, wade, climb and flounder over No Man's Land to visit my other post. It took me half an hour to move about 150 yards.

I was chiefly annoyed by our own machine guns from behind. The
35   seeng-seeng-seeng of the bullets reminded me of Mary's canary. On the whole I can support the canary better.

In the Platoon on my left the sentries over the dug-out were blown to nothing. One of these poor fellows was my first servant whom I rejected. If I had kept him he would have lived, for servants don't do Sentry Duty.
40   I kept my own sentries half way down the stairs during the more terrific bombardment. In spite of this one lad was blown down and, I am afraid, blinded.

What passing-bells for these who die as cattle?
  Only the monstrous anger of the guns.
45   Only the stuttering rifles' rapid rattle
Can patter out their hasty orisons.
No mockeries now for them; no prayers nor bells,
  Nor any voice of mourning save the choirs,—
The shrill demented choirs of wailing shells;
50   And bugles calling for them from sad shires.

What candles may be held to speed them all?
  Not in the hands of boys, but in their eyes
Shall shine the holy glimmers of good-byes.
  The pallor of girls' brows shall be their pall;
55 Their flowers the tenderness of patient minds,
And each slow dusk a drawing-down of blinds.

Wilfred Owen, 'Anthem for Doomed Youth'
Letter and poem in J. Stallworthy (ed.)*Poets of the First World War*
OUP/Imperial War Museum, 1974, pp. 13–15

Questions

a What features of trench warfare are vividly portrayed by Owen in his letter?

b Which aspects of this picture were most likely to cause emotional strain on the participants?

c Comment on the literary techniques used by Owen in his poem.

d One critic wrote that from Owen's poems we receive 'that exalted pleasure, that sense of being lifted above the sphere of anger and despair . . . the calm is unmistakeable.' Is this so of this poem?

* e How has the war poetry of 1917 changed from that of the first year of war, for example, 'The Dead' by Rupert Brooke?

* f Was there poetry of a comparable quality and quantity written during the Second World War?

5 Scientific Intelligence

Two or three nights before the bombing of London started on 7th September [1940], my sleep was interrupted. . . . This was the telephone . . . ringing in the small hours of the morning and an excited voice saying, 'This is Norman at Bletchley. We've got something new
5 here. God knows what it is, but I'm sure it's something for you!' . . .
    The cryptographers had broken a new line of Enigma traffic. There were mentions of beams, including one which said that the beam width was eight to ten seconds of arc, or an angle of one in twenty thousand, which would imply that the beam was no wider than twenty yards at two

hundred miles. And there was the electrifying word 'X-GERÄT' which was being fitted to an aircraft with a call sign 6N +LK, which identified it as belonging to Kampf Gruppe 100. The unit had attempted to attack Birmingham on 13th/14th August. . . . I quickly correlated the new beams with those which Scott-Farnie told me had just begun to be heard on frequencies around 70 Megacycles per second from the Cherbourg and Calais areas. . . .

So the X-Gerät was indeed something distinct from Knickebein. . . . By 24th September we had identified six beams . . . and we had the exact positions of the first two which were again on the Hague peninsula north-west of Cherbourg. The next three were near Calais, and the last near Brest. Kampf Gruppe 100 seemed to be working in somewhat irregular order through a book of numbered targets, and the chief scientist involved appeared to be a Dr Kühnhold. We had the actual directions for the beams for 20th September . . . implying an aiming accuracy of about ten yards at two hundred miles. . . .

Could such accuracy be attained with the radio waves of frequencies around 70 Megacycles per second that I had already associated with the X-Gerät . . . or would it require still shorter wavelengths of, say, less than a metre? The Germans talked of coarse and fine beams, and the 70 Megacycle beams might be the coarse ones only. Further, there were mentions of centimetres in the Enigma messages. I had already been alarmed by the fact that we had no listening receivers for centimetric waves where . . . German radar might well be, so I used the centimetric beam possibility as a lever to get a special listening watch on these wavelengths across the Straits of Dover. . . . It was almost immediately fruitful for they detected radar-type transmissions on a wavelength of 80 centimetres. . . .

I had recommended on 11th September that similar countermeasures to those . . . against Knickebein should be developed against the X-beams. . . . However, they did not seem to have much effect on KGr 100 which continued to bomb more or less as it pleased. . . .

If only we could decode the Enigma messages in time, we could find where and when KGr 100 was going to attack, and so counter them by having fighters waiting and by having our jamming ready on the right frequencies. This would make great demands on the codebreakers, for the orders did not go out to the beam stations until the afternoon, giving only two or three hours to make the break. But for such a prize they strained every resource of human intelligence and endurance; and it was a great day, late in October, when they achieved this fantastic feat for the first time. Thereafter, they were able to repeat it on about one night in three. I was then able (having first worked out the position of the cross-beam stations near Calais) to tell the Duty Air Commodore at Fighter Command the exact place of attack, the time of the first bomb to within ten minutes or so, the expected ground speed of the bombers, their line of approach to within 100 yards, and their height to within two or three hundred metres. Could any air defence system ask for more? . . .

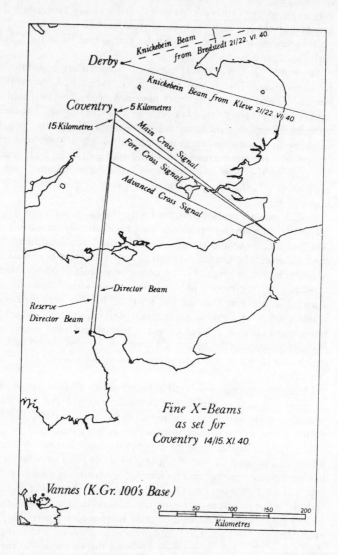

The X-Beam dispositions for the bombing of Coventry on 14/15 November 1940. Also shown are two Knickebein beams focused on Derby, for the night of 21/22 June 1940

Scientific Intelligence was now [1941] established as a branch having
its place alongside and interlocked with the more traditional divisions of
60 Naval, Military and Air Intelligence, and we had the beginnings of a
Scientific Intelligence organization. I had been able to share in the effort
by the relatively small band of scientists and engineers which had affected
the outcome of the Battle of Britain and the Blitz. Beyond its effect on the
immediate outcome it had made a great difference to the position of
65 science in national affairs, for it had shown the government . . . that
science and engineering could be essential to national survival. . . .

R.V. Jones, *Most Secret War*, Hamish Hamilton (Hodder &
Stoughton edn 1979), 1978 pp. 186-7, 189-93, 240-41

Questions

a From internal evidence, what were the general functions of
   'Knickebein' (line 18) and 'X-Gerät' (line 10)?
b How was so much information available on this subject, and what was
   the connection with 'Enigma' (line 6)?
c What action could be taken against 'X-Gerät'?
d Comment on the effectiveness of Scientific Intelligence to the war
   effort on the basis of this evidence.
* e The map shows the dispositions for the raid on Coventry. What
      happened to this city, and why is there still controversy about it?
* f How could the developments in science and engineering in wartime
      be applied once the war was over?

6 Atomic Energy

The year of the outbreak of the Second World War was . . . a year of
dramatic advance in nuclear physics and this coincidence of circumstance
was to form a watershed in history. . . . The scientific journals were full
of the notes and articles describing the rapid succession of discoveries that
5 had at last made the release of atomic energy from uranium a possibility,
albeit a remote one. . . . The fundamentally important article by Bohr
and Wheeler explaining the fission process . . . was published only two
days before the outbreak of war. . . .

Knowledge had reached the point where several groups of scientists in
10 different countries were reporting almost similar experiments or taking
almost identical strides in theory at almost the same moment. Discoveries
in these circumstances could not be hidden. . . . Internationalism still
ruled in science and fundamental discoveries were being made by
Germans who still lived in Nazi Germany, by German, Italian,
15 Hungarian and Austrian scientists who had fled their countries, by
Frenchmen, by Danes and by Americans. . . .

In the spring of 1939, as the scientists explained that the nucleus of the
uranium atom could be split, that an enormous amount of energy would
be released in the fission and that a chain fission reaction was a possibility,

20 the inevitable question had arisen. Could this energy be harnessed for
making a super bomb?. . . .

Two prospects came into view: one peaceful, the steady and
continuous output of energy in a suitable form for use in a prime mover,
and the other destructive, an explosive of almost inconceivable violence.
25 The fact that the climax of the discoveries came in 1939 . . . made it
'inevitable' that many of the best physicists in Britain should spend their
efforts in realising the destructive potentialities of nuclear energy. Unless
they were pacifists, there was no other choice before them.

M. M. Gowing, *Britain and Atomic Energy 1939—1945*, Macmillan,
1964, pp. 33—4, 88—9

The first successful nuclear chain reaction was conducted under the old
30 west stands of the University of Chicago's football stadium. A graphite-
moderated uranium pile was constructed under strict wartime secrecy.
The director was an Italian emigré named Enrico Fermi, forced to leave
Italy by the rising tide of fascism in the late 1930s. The pile was
constructed of graphite bricks in which were embedded plugs of natural
35 uranium. A clandestine photograph taken in November 1942 . . . shows
alternating layers of all graphite blocks . . . and graphite blocks embedded with uranium slugs. . . . At 57 layers the pile became critical, or
capable of sustaining a chain reaction. Gary Sheehan, the staff artist for the
Chicago *Tribune*, recreated the December 2, 1942 scene, 'The Day
40 Tomorrow Began', depicting the dramatic, first test. The three standing
on top of the pile . . . were referred to as the suicide squad. It was their
job to flood the pile with a solution of cadmium salt in case things got out
of hand among the fissioning uranium nuclei inside the pile. Cadmium is
an excellent neutron absorber. At the base of the pile is a lone man
45 controlling a long cadmium rod whose removal from the pile allowed a
gradual approach to the self-sustaining state. Without that cadmium rod
absorbing neutrons, the pile would go out of control. In fact, rumor [*sic*]
has it that in typical army fashion, there was a cover story ready to be
released about some large arsenal blowing up accidentally, if the pile
50 didn't quite work properly and a chunk of Chicago went up in what
would have been the first nuclear explosion. But all went well. The key
figure in the painting is Fermi himself, the 'Italian navigator', standing on
the balcony ordering the calculated withdrawals of the control rod. An
oscilloscope record of the neutron intensity showed the exponential rise
55 in the curve that was achieved between 3:00 and 3:30 p.m. indicating the
reaction to be self-sustaining. Here was one of the great discoveries of
modern science and it could not be announced to the world because of the
wartime crisis. Publication consisted of a single telephone message, in
cryptogram, that read, 'The Italian navigator has landed in the new
60 world. The natives are friendly.' The test of CP-1 (Chicago Pile-1) was a
success.

L. Fine, *Chemistry Decoded*, OUP, 1976, pp. 233—4

Questions

a What were a 'nuclear chain reaction' (line 29) and a 'uranium pile' (line 31)?

b Why was 1939 an important year for nuclear physics?

c Explain the importance of 2 December 1942 in the development of nuclear research. Why was it 'The Day Tomorrow Began' (lines 39–40)?

* *d* What part was played in 'Tube Alloys' and the 'Manhattan Project' by British scientists? Why was the research concentrated on the United States?

* *e* 'I am become death, the destroyer of worlds.' Discuss the use of the atomic bomb on Japan in 1945.

* *f* Examine the 'two prospects' (line 22) of nuclear energy as they developed in Britain after the Second World War.

7 The Second World War: Change or Continuity?

The impact of the war on British domestic history. . . is extraordinarily difficult to determine, for any attempt to draw up an assessment involves us at once in problems of hypothesis. If the war had not occurred, what would have happened in the six years, 1939 to 1945 . . . Too frequently
5 it was assumed, at the end of the war or shortly afterwards, that changes which had occurred since 1939 were the direct outcome of the war. As time goes by. . . we are able to get a clearer picture of the long-term trends, and in many cases we then discover that what people have ascribed to the impact of war really has more deep-seated causes. All too often the
10 observer has failed to avoid the commonest of historical pitfalls, the fallacy of *post hoc, ergo propter hoc*. . . .

A. T. Peacock and J. Wiseman have argued that war has a 'displacement effect, shifting public revenues and expenditures to new levels'. They claim that this is partly because the crisis of war enables levels
15 of taxation to be raised, and it is easier to keep up an existing rate of taxation in peacetime than to raise it for the first time. . . . At the same time, wars are inclined to raise social problems which governments feel they must spend money in solving. Peacock and Wiseman speak of this as an 'inspection effect'. . . .
20 The main difficulty. . . is that there is no reason to suppose that, in the absence of total war, government expenditure would have remained constant as a proportion of the gross national product. In Britain there was a rapid increase of expenditure in the years 1900 to 1914, and there has been a considerable increase again in the years since 1955. . . .
25 If . . . we examine separately the expansion of the social services, we find that the growth of expenditure per head . . . has been remarkably uniform since the beginning of the century. . . .

The stresses and strains of war transformed ordinary family life, but it is surprising how little difference they made in the long run. By mid-1944
30 about 30 per cent of the male working population were in the forces and

for most of them this meant separation from their wives, parents, children, homes. Many civilian families were also split up for long periods, owing to the evacuation of mothers and children from the cities. . . . Women's work also altered the character of family life:
35 comparing 1943 with 1939, about three million more women had become engaged in . . . work. . . .

On balance, the nation's health was surprisingly good. The death rates did not appreciably increase, and maternal mortality fell markedly. . . the most important single factor was probably the im-
40 provement in family incomes. . . .

In the hectic days of 1940, it was quite common for people to suppose that the war was effecting a social revolution in Britain. Many of the wealthy thought so, and lamented that they had lived to go through such an experience. . . .
45 Undoubtedly the war brought into existence for a time a stronger sense of community throughout the country. . . . Dunkirk, the Battle of Britain and the Blitz produced a 'backs-to-the-wall' solidarity that transcended class barriers and brought together all sorts of people in the Home Guard, Civil Defence, the air raid shelters and . . . to some extent
50 the factories. . . . The increased mobility of the population . . . tended to break down parochialism. . . .

In spite of the shocks of 1940, the Second World War made much less of an impact on the British mind than the First War had done. In 1914 the country was not prepared mentally for the trials that it had to undergo –
55 the appalling suffering of the trenches and a rate of casualties never previously experienced. But in 1939 most people feared a repetition of the First World War, and so there was no psychological trauma resulting from the sacrifices that it eventually involved. . . .

There had not been much of that 'inspection effect'. . . or, if there had
60 been, it had found most institutions not unsatisfactory, and so served to reinforce the view which so many people in Britain still retained: that somehow or other, things in their own country were arranged much better than elsewhere in the world – even if, in limited directions only, there might be some room for improvement.

H. Pelling, *Britain and the Second World War*, Collins/Fontana, 1970, pp. 297–9, 303–4, 320–22, 325–6

Questions

a What is the 'fallacy of *post hoc, ergo propter hoc*' (line 11)?
b How does Pelling develop the point made in the first paragraph when examining government expenditure, family life, and medical improvements?
c Examine the distinction made between short and long term social effects of the war.
* d Compare Pelling's views with those of Marwick in document I. Is there much difference between them?

e   Is it true to say that 'there was no psychological trauma' (line 57) resulting from the Second World War?

*   f   Discuss the comment that it was the Second World War which helped the Labour Party into power to carry out its programme of far-reaching social reforms.

Further Work

a   Discuss R. Titmuss' comment that 'the aims and content of social policy, both in peace and in war, are . . . determined — at least to a substantial extent — by how far the co-operation of the masses is essential to the successful prosecution of the war.'

b   Considering the growing liberation of women in the First World War, discuss the view that 'the ordinary male disbelief in our capacity cannot be argued away, it can only be worked away.' (Dr Elsie Inglis)

c   Other than the examples in this chapter, where can the impact of the two world wars be seen in the history of Britain in the twentieth century?

II 'The Damnable Question' — the Insoluble Issue of Ireland

Introduction

It is not surprising that George Dangerfield should have taken the statement made by Asquith about Ireland being that 'damnable question' as the title for his recent book which looks at the Irish question between 1916 and 1921. The question remains and seems to be as insoluble today as it was in 1916–21. The 1960s marked a watershed both for Northern Ireland and for the historians' perceptions of the Irish question. The events of the late 1960s and the 1970s destroyed the political formula which had been used to contain the Irish problem since the 1920s. It is something of an irony that just as events in Ireland were leading to the suspension of the United Kingdom's first experiment with a devolved system of internal self-government, Scotland and Wales were showing a resurgence of nationalism and advancing claims for a separate treatment from the rest of the United Kingdom. Home Rule or devolution is as much an issue of the eighties as it was of the 1910s and 1920s.

Between the Act of Union of 1800 and the Irish Treaty of 1921 the whole of Ireland was an integral part of the United Kingdom, although the colonisation of Ireland had begun long before 1800. The spread of Irish nationalism in the mid and especially late nineteenth century, Gladstone's attempts to give Home Rule and the passage of the Parliament Act in 1911 made some form of devolution inevitable in Ireland. The position of the Protestants of Ulster — no more than 27 per cent of the total population — and their willingness to resist any settlement in which they would be left as a small minority meant that any solution was likely to be accompanied by violence. Indeed, on the eve of the First World War it was apparent that Ulster's Protestant population would resist Home Rule if need be by force of arms and the Curragh Mutiny indicated that the army might not repress rebellion.

War in Europe in 1914 led to Home Rule being shelved. The result was the Easter rebellion of 1916, when for a bloody week central Dublin was a battlefield. The 1916 Proclamation indicates the aims of the insurgents — nationalistic but idealistic. The Rising had little popular support but, as John Dillon argued, the executions which followed in May infuriated the Irish population and led to Asquith accepting that some political solution was necessary. The question of partition from the Ulster Unionist point of view is considered in the letter from Hugh De F. Montgomery. To discuss this problem and to try and find a solution of a moderate nature a Convention was called in 1917. Its meetings were boycotted by both organised labour and Sinn Fein and any attempt at solution was blocked in the conference chamber by the total refusal of the Ulster Unionists to consider the possibility of Home Rule for the whole of Ireland. This meant that partition was now the only possible solution, with all the problems which are still apparent today. In 1920, in an atmosphere of civil disorder in Ireland, Parliament passed the Government of Ireland Act providing for separate Home Rule Parliaments, for six northern counties at Belfast and for the remaining twenty-six counties in Dublin. This was followed by civil war in the South which led to the Anglo-Irish treaty of 1921 by which the South became a dominion, albeit a restless one, until in 1949 it became an independent republic outside the Commonwealth. Meanwhile, Ulster operated the devolved institutions conferred upon it by the Act until it was suspended in 1972.

The legacy of the Easter Rebellion lived on. According to Liam de Paor and Conor Cruise O'Brien, 1966 was a watershed in the relationship between the two communities in Northern Ireland: that year was the anniversary of the Easter Rebellion which, for the Catholic population, symbolised the ideal of a united Ireland. The celebrations which accompanied this fiftieth anniversary led to a backlash from the Ulster Protestants who remembered 1916 not as the year of the Easter Rising, but as the year in which Ulster divisions were cut to pieces on the Somme. The problem of Ireland still remains. The basic character of the problem is the same today as it was in 1916. The legacy of history persists. The historian's task is made more difficult by the problems of subjectivity and distortion which pervade both primary and secondary material on the subject. In the study of Irish history the writer is often an advocate rather than an impartial but involved commentator. The mythology of the past still prevents a lasting solution to the colonial dilemma.

Further Reading

Useful information on the history of Ireland leading up to 1920 and beyond can be found in:

J. C. Becket, *The Making of Modern Ireland 1603–1923* (Faber, 1969)

F. S. L. Lyons, *Ireland Since the Famine* (Fontana, 1973, rev. edn 1974), undoubtedly the most comprehensive study of Ireland, both north and south, from 1846; excellent bibliography.

N. Mansergh, *The Irish Question 1840–1921* (Allen and Unwin, 1965)

J. A. Murphy, *Ireland in the Twentieth Century* (Gill and Macmillan, 1975), a good study of the twentieth century.

On the 1916 Rising and the events leading up to partition in 1920 see:

O. D. Edwards and F. Pyle, *1916: The Easter Rising* (MacGibbon & Kee, 1968)

R. B. McDowell, *The Irish Convention, 1917–18* (London, 1970) a detailed study of a neglected and important topic.

F. X. Martin (ed.), *Leaders and Men of the Easter Rising: Dublin, 1916* (Methuen, 1967), a good biographical approach.

* K. B. Nowlan (ed.), *The Making of 1916: studies in the history of The Rising* (Stationery Office, Dublin, 1969)

A. T. Q. Stewart, *The Ulster Crisis* (Faber, 1967)

On the situation since 1920 in addition to the excellent, if partisan, work by Liam de Paor, the following are worthy of mention:
* B. Chubb, *The Government and Politics of Ireland* (Oxford, 1970)

R. Rose, *Governing Without Consensus* (London, 1971)

Northern Ireland: a Time for Choice (London, 1976)
* J. H. Whyte, *Church and State in Northern Ireland 1923–1970* (Macmillan, 1971), a comprehensive treatment of the problem.

On the revival of nationalism in other parts of the United Kingdom as well as Ireland the following studies are crucial:

A. H. Birch, *Political Integration and Disintegration in the British Isles* (Allen and Unwin, 1967)

V. Bogdanor, *Devolution* (Oxford University Press, 1979), the best general discussion of the problem which has much to say on Ireland.

Additional documentary material can be obtained in a work published too late to be fully considered in this chapter:

Grenfell Morton, *Home Rule and the Irish Question* (Longman, Seminar Studies in History, 1980), a good study of the nineteenth-century background to this chapter with 44 documents excellently chosen.

1   Rebellion

POBLACHT NA EIREANN
THE PROVISIONAL GOVERNMENT
OF THE
IRISH REPUBLIC
5   TO THE PEOPLE OF IRELAND

IRISHMEN AND IRISHWOMEN: In the name of God and of the dead generations from which she receives her old tradition of nationhood, Ireland, through us, summons her children to her flag and strikes for her freedom.

10   Having organized her manhood through her secret revolutionary organization, the Irish Republican Brotherhood, and through her open military organizations, the Irish Volunteers and the Irish Citizen Army, having patiently perfected her discipline, having resolutely waited for the right moment to reveal herself, she now seizes that moment, and
15 supported by her exiled children in America and by gallant allies in Europe, but relying in the first on her own strength, she strikes in full confidence of victory.

We declare the right of the people of Ireland to the ownership of Ireland and to the unfettered control of Irish destinies, to be sovereign and
20 indefeasible. The long usurpation of that right by a foreign people and government has not extinguished that right, nor can it ever be extinguished except by the destruction of the Irish people. In every generation the Irish people have asserted their right to national freedom

and sovereignty; six times during the past three hundred years they have
25 asserted it in arms. Standing on that fundamental right and again asserting
it in arms in the face of the world, we hereby proclaim the Irish Republic
as a Sovereign Independent State, and we pledge our lives and the lives of
our comrades in arms to the cause of its freedom, of its welfare and of its
exaltation among the nations.
30   The Irish Republic is entitled to, and hereby claims, the allegiance of
every Irishman and Irishwoman. The Republic guarantees religious and
civil liberty, equal rights and equal opportunities to all its citizens, and
declares its resolve to pursue the happiness and prosperity of the whole
nation and of all its parts, cherishing all the children of the nation equally,
35 and oblivious of the differences carefully fostered by an alien
Government, which have divided a minority from the majority in the
past.
        We place the cause of the Irish Republic under the protection of the
Most High God, Whose blessing we invoke under our arms, and we pray
40 that no one who serves that cause will dishonour it by cowardice,
inhumanity or rapine. In this supreme hour the Irish nation must, by its
valour and discipline, and by the readiness of its children to sacrifice
themselves for the common good, prove itself worthy of the august
destiny to which it is called.
45   Signed on behalf of the Provisional Government:

Thomas J. Clarke,

Sean MacDiarmida	*Thomas MacDonagh*
P. H. Pearse,	*Eamonn Ceannt,*
James Connolly,	*Joseph Plunkett.*

The 1916 Proclamation is printed in F. S. L. Lyons *Ireland Since
the Famine*, Fontana edn 1978, pp. 369−70

Questions

a   (i) What is the significance of lines 6−8 for the document as a whole?
    (ii) What was the 'Irish Republican Brotherhood' (line 11) and why
    was it important?
    (iii) Explain the meaning of lines 15−16.
    (iv) What does 'sovereign and indefeasible' (lines 19−20) mean?
    (v) On what 'six times during the past three hundred years' did 'the
    Irish people' assert 'in arms' their right to self-rule (lines 24−5)?
    (vi) Explain the meaning of lines 35−7.
*   b   Who were the signatories of the Proclamation? Find out about them
    and their ideas.
c   The vague nature of the 1916 Proclamation reflects the poor
    organisation of the Easter Rebellion. Discuss.
d   How did the 1916 Proclamation attempt to deal with the deep social
    and religious divisions in Ireland? Do you think its solutions were
    convincing?

* *e* The idealism of 1916 is clearly reflected in the Proclamation. It was an idealism with a long historical tradition. How viable was Irish nationalism as an alternative government in 1916?

2   1916 – the reaction of John Dillon

I admit they were wrong; I know they were wrong; but they fought a clean fight, and they fought with superb bravery and skill, and no act of savagery or act against the usual custom of war that I know of has been brought home to any leader or any organized body of insurgents. . . .
5   As a matter of fact the great bulk of the population were not favourable to the insurrection, and the insurgents themselves, who had confidently counted on a rising of the people in their support, were absolutely disappointed. They got no popular support whatever. What is happening is that thousands of people in Dublin, who ten days ago were bitterly
10 opposed to the whole of the Sinn Fein movement and to the rebellion are now becoming infuriated against the Government on account of these executions and, as I am informed by letters received this morning, that feeling is spreading throughout the country in a most dangerous degree. . . .
15 We who speak for the vast majority of the Irish people, we who have risked a great deal to win the people to your side in this great crisis of your Empire's history, we who have endeavoured, and successfully endeavoured to secure that the Irish in America shall not go into alliance with the Germans in that country – we, I think, were entitled to be
20 consulted before this bloody course of executions was entered upon in Ireland.

> Hansard, 5th ser., vol. 82, cols 945, 950, printed in Grenfell Morton, *Home Rule and the Irish Question*, Longman, 1980, pp. 110–11

Questions

a   (i) What was 'the usual custom of war' (line 3)?
(ii) What was 'the Sinn Fein movement' (line 10) and what was its importance in the history of Ireland?
(iii) What were 'these executions' (lines 12–13)?
(iv) What was 'this great crisis of your Empire's history' (lines 16–17)?
* *b*   Who was John Dillon and what part did he play in the history of Ireland in the early twentieth century?
c   What information can be obtained from this speech about the popularity of the Easter Rebellion?
d   What does Dillon see as a consequence for the insurgents of the government's policy? Was he correct in his conclusions?
e   The success of the Easter Rebellion lay in the creation of additional nationalist martyrs. It achieved little else. Discuss.

3 Partition

It took Carson an hour and a half to explain the situation at the private
meeting of the Unionist Council, and I cannot pretend to tell you all he
told us; but the main point was this— The Cabinet having unanimously
decided that under the pressure of difficulties with America, the Colonies
5 and Parliament (but chiefly with America) they must offer Redmond
Home Rule at once; and (not being prepared to coerce Ulster) having
authorised Lloyd George to arrange a settlement, Carson, after what had
happened at the Buckingham Palace Conference in 1914, could not well
refuse to submit to his followers the exclusion of six counties as a basis of
10 negotiation. Carson had satisfied himself, apparently, that he had lost all
the ground he and his colleagues had gained in their anti-Home Rule
campaign before the war, and that the majority of the Unionist members
and voters took the same view as the majority of Unionist papers as to the
necessity of a settlement . . . . If we did not agree to a settlement we
15 should have the Home Rule Act coming into operation without the
exclusion of any part of Ulster, or subject only to some worthless
Amending Act which Asquith might bring in in fulfilment of his pledge,
and we should either have to submit to this or fight . . . . I was in Dublin
for two or three days last week, and the Southerners I met are all
20 convinced that there will be another rebellion whether the Lloyd George
terms are accepted or not. The fact that these terms were suggested has
enormously strengthened the Sinn Feiners in the country. The acceptance
of the suggestions by the Ulster Unionists has not had much effect on this
part of the question. The Unionists' acceptance under protest has only
25 increased Redmond's difficulties, and, as we are given to believe, placed
us in the position in the eyes of British public opinion of being reasonable
people. If Redmond actually forms a government and tries to rule this
country, the rebellion will be directed against him; if he does not, it will
be directed against the existing government: in any case, the country will
30 have to be more or less conquered outside the six counties, and that may
possibly be the best way out of all our troubles, which have all their root
in a British Prime Minister having brought in a Home Rule Bill.

> Extract from a letter of Hugh De F. Montgomery, of the Ulster
> Unionist Council, to his son, dated 22 June 1916; Montgomery
> Papers NIPRO D627/429.

Questions

a (i) Who were Carson (line 1) and the Unionist Council (line 2) and
what part did they play in the politics of Ireland in the 1910s?
(ii) Who was Redmond (line 5) and what part did he play in the
history of Ireland to 1918?
(iii) What were 'the six counties' (line 9)?
(iv) Who were 'the Southerners' (line 19)?
(v) Explain the significance of lines 30–2.

* b In what ways had the attitude of the Ulster Unionists changed
between 1913 and 1916 and why?

c What does Montgomery see as the result of the Home Rule Act? Was he correct in his conclusions?

* *d* Partition was viewed by the Ulster Unionists as the lesser of two evils. They were not fully committed to it. Discuss.

* *e* Compare Ulster and Irish nationalism in the early twentieth century.

4 The Government of Ireland Act, 1920

1 (1) On and after the appointed day there shall be established for Southern Ireland a parliament to be called the parliament of Southern Ireland consisting of His Majesty, the Senate of Southern Ireland, and the House of Commons of Southern Ireland, and there shall be established for
5 Northern Ireland a parliament to be called the parliament of Northern Ireland consisting of His Majesty, the Senate of Northern Ireland and the House of Commons of Northern Ireland.

(2) For the purpose of this act, Northern Ireland shall consist of the parliamentary counties of Antrim, Armagh, Down, Fermanagh, Lon-
10 donderry and Tyrone, and the parliamentary boroughs of Belfast and Londonderry, and Southern Ireland shall consist of so much of Ireland as is not comprised within the said parliamentary counties and boroughs.

2 (1) With a view to the eventual establishment of a parliament for the whole of Ireland, and to bringing about harmonization between the
15 parliaments and governments of Southern Ireland and Northern Ireland, and to the promotion of mutual intercourse and uniformity in relation to matters affecting the whole of Ireland, and to providing for the administration of services which the two parliaments mutually agree should be administered uniformly throughout the whole of Ireland, or
20 which by virtue of this Act are to be so administered, there shall be constituted as soon as may be after the appointed day a council to be called the Council of Ireland.

(2) Subject as hereinafter provided, the Council of Ireland shall consist of a person nominated by the Lord Lieutenant acting in accordance with
25 instructions from His Majesty who shall be president, and forty other persons, of whom seven shall be members of the Senate of Southern Ireland, thirteen shall be members of the House of Commons of Southern Ireland, seven shall be members of the Senate of Northern Ireland, and thirteen shall be members of the House of Commons of Northern
30 Ireland . . . .

4 (1) Subject to the provisions of this act, the Parliament of Southern Ireland and the Parliament of Northern Ireland shall respectively have power to make laws for peace, order and good government of Southern Ireland and Northern Ireland with the following limitations, namely,
35 that they shall not have power to make laws except in respect of matters exclusively relating to the portion of Ireland within their jurisdiction, or some part thereof, and (without prejudice to that general limitation) that

they shall not have power to make laws in respect of the following
matters in particular: the crown, war and peace, foreign trade . . . .

40 **5** (1) In the exercise of their power to make laws under this act neither
the Parliament of Southern Ireland nor the Parliament of Northern
Ireland shall make a law so as either directly or indirectly to establish or
endow any religion, or prohibit or restrict the free exercise thereof, or
give a preference, privilege or advantage, or impose any disability or
45 disadvantage, on account of religious belief . . . .

75 Notwithstanding the establishment of the Parliaments of Southern
and Northern Ireland, or the Parliament of Ireland . . . the supreme
authority of the Parliament of the United Kingdom shall remain
unaffected . . . .

Extracts from the Government of Ireland Act 1920 (10 and 11
Geo. V, ch. 6, 7)

Questions

a What was the constitutional structure of Northern.and Southern
Ireland to be like as a result of this Act?
* b How far was the constitutional structure set up in 1920 an attempt to
satisfy the aspirations of the differing groups in Irish society? Did it
succeed?
c How did the 1920 Act deal with the question of religion?
d Given the attitudes of the Ulstermen in the 1960s towards Catholics
and the discrimination against Catholics, how successful do you think
the religious clause in the 1920 Act was?
e The Government of Ireland Act 1920 has to be considered in relation
to the Anglo-Irish 'Treaty' of 1921. Discuss.
* f In what ways was this experiment in devolution a success?
* g What determined the reaction of (a) British politicians and (b) the
British people to the crisis?

5   1916—an Irish View

In Northern Ireland Catholics are Blacks who happen to have white
skins. This is not a truth. It is an oversimplification and too facile an
analogy. But it is a better oversimplification than that which sees the
struggle and conflict in Northern Ireland in terms of religion. Catholics
5 and Protestants are not quarrelling with one another (most of them)
because of matters of theology or faith. . . . The Northern Ireland
problem is a colonial problem, and the 'racial' distinction (and it is
actually imagined as racial) between the colonists and the natives is
expressed in terms of religion. It goes perhaps somewhat deeper than that;
10 for it is necessary to maintain the distinction in order to maintain the

colony as a colony. It is true that the colonizing of Northern Ireland took place a long time ago; it is true that there was a time when it seemed that distinctions might be merged in a happy integration of the descendants of the settlers with the descendants of the natives, but for historical reasons this tendency was reversed almost two centuries ago, and it has always since seemed to be to the advantage of somebody to keep Ulster divided.

Pearse and his I. R. B. comrades, who broke with Redmond . . . did not feel that they owed any loyalty to England or that they should fight her wars. On the contrary they hoped that the great European war might provide an opportunity to strike against the colonial connection, and they planned accordingly. Connolly, with his tiny Citizen Army, was even more opposed to Irishmen fighting, not only in England's, but in any capitalist war, and he was bitterly disappointed to see Europe's socialist parties forgetting their principles when the drums beat and the banners waved, and hastening to wear the uniforms of Europe's various oppressors on both sides. He too was a nationalist of a kind, although he had made it clear that he was not interested in a mere change of flags but in attacking capitalism through colonialism. He too prepared to strike, and early in 1916 he worked out an agreement with the Volunteers to cooperate with them.

The plans for an uprising throughout the country in 1916 went badly awry—and even at best their hopes of success depended on moral rather than military considerations. . . . An effective force turned out only in Dublin, on Easter Monday, and even there it was far below strength; nevertheless the authorities were taken by surprise and the Volunteers and Citizen Army seized the centre of the city and held it with great courage for a bloody week against the British army. . . . Eventually, after shelling and burning had reduced their strong-points, the insurgents surrendered, leaving Dublin in ruins . . . and Ireland changed. In the early days of May, morning after morning, the leaders of the rising were shot in Kilmainham jail, stunning with reiterated shock the minds of a population who had known these men. . . .

On 1 July the battle of the Somme opened, and the 36th (Ulster) Division was ordered out of their section of the British lines at Thiepval Wood on the River Ancre to attack the German lines. They attacked with tremendous courage . . . and in two days of battle . . . ended more or less where they had begun, in terms of ground gained. But their dead were heaped in thousands on the German wire and littered the ground that had been bitterly gained and bitterly lost: half of Ulster was in mourning.

These two bloody events drove Irishmen further apart than ever, for although the Catholic and nationalist Irish also, 200,000 of them, fought, and many died, at the Somme, at Gallipoli, at Passchendaele, and other places with names of terror in that appalling war, their sacrifice seemed, by the turn Irish history now took, irrelevant—barely a footnote in the developing myth by which the political tradition is animated:

It was England bade our wild geese go
That small nations might be free:
60   Their lonely graves are by Suvla's wave
Or the fringe of the great North Sea;
But had they died by Pearse's side
Or fallen by Cathal Brugha
Their graves we'd keep where the Fenians sleep
65   With a shroud of the foggy dew.

In Ulster, on the other hand, the Somme is more central in the Protestant political tradition, for, futile as the battle was, the Orangemen who fought in it displayed in the most convincing way that, however eccentric their 'loyalty' might seem at times, it was to them quite real, and 70 they showed that in this they were, as Pearse had perceived, not ridiculous at all. . . .

Asquith himself, in the aftermath of the Dublin Easter rising, under pressure from America because of the executions, stopped General Maxwell, the military commander in Dublin from shooting his prisoners, 75 and announced to the House of Commons on 11 May:

The government has come to the conclusion that the system under which Ireland has been governed has completely broken down. The only satisfactory alternative, in their judgement, is the creation, at the earliest possible moment, of an Irish Government responsible to the Irish people.

80 He went to Ireland, returned, and told parliament that the government had asked Lloyd George to negotiate for 'agreement as to the way in which the Government of Ireland is for the future to be carried out', so that the home rule bill might be put into effect immediately, without waiting for the end of the war. . . . The Government of Ireland Act, 85 1920, was a dead letter, so far as the greater part of the country was concerned. One part of it, however, was already in effect; one part of the new Irish settlement had been made: Ireland was partitioned; Ulster was partitioned. A settlement desired and welcomed by no party in Ireland had been imposed.

    Liam de Paor, *Divided Ulster*, Penguin edn 1971, pp. xii—xiv, 81—3, 90

Questions

a   (i) In what ways was 'The Northern Ireland problem . . . a colonial problem' (lines 6—7)?
(ii) Explain the importance of lines 13—15 to an understanding of the Irish problem.
(iii) Who were Pearse (line 18) and Connolly (line 22)? In what ways did their ideas about Ireland differ?
(iv) Explain lines 24—7.
(v) What do lines 33—4 tell you about the Dublin Rising?
(vi) Why did 'pressure from America' stop the executions (line 73)?

(vii) 'Ireland was partitioned; Ulster was partitioned' (lines 87–8). Comment.

b   How valid do you think Liam de Paor's interpretation of the 1916 Rising and the problem of Ireland is? In what ways does it exhibit biased judgement?

* c   The key to understanding the problem of Ireland in 1916 or in 1980 is historical. But the history of Ireland is used by all protagonists to justify their positions. Does this preclude any real historical analysis of the problem?

d   What value is the extract from a republican ballad (lines 58–65) as historical evidence?

e   The history of Ireland since 1916 has been determined by the Dublin Rising and the Somme. Discuss.

* f   Could partition have been avoided in 1920? Was there any alternative?

Further Work

a   Religion is merely one facet of the Irish problem. Discuss.

b   Consider the histories of Northern Ireland and Southern Ireland since 1920. In what ways do they differ?

c   Disraeli once wrote that 'England is not governed by logic but by Parliament'. How logical was the Irish solution in 1920–21?

d   Since 1969 the historian's perception of the Irish solution of 1920–21 has altered. Discuss.

e   A society may be held together through what Gladstone called a 'recognition of the distinctive qualities of the separate parts of great countries'. If this answer is correct, devolution will strengthen national unity, not weaken it. Discuss this in relation to Ireland since 1916.

f   Why has there been a revival of nationalism and demands for devolution since 1970?

III 'Between the Devil and the Deep Blue Sea' — the Liberal Dilemma and the Party's Decline, 1914—35

Introduction

The Liberal governments of Campbell-Bannerman and Asquith initiated, between 1906 and 1914, a series of social and political reforms of a far-reaching character. Yet by 1935 the Liberal Party was reduced to 21 MPs. This dramatic change of fortune is the subject of this chapter. The emphasis is placed upon the period 1914—22 in identifying the basic reasons for Liberal decline and for the Liberal dilemma which persists to the present.

Whether Dangerfield's idea of the 'strange death of Liberal England' between 1910 and 1914 is a valid thesis is still strongly debated by historians. Its significance lies not in its basic idea, called by Ross McKibbin 'a literary confection', but in its identification of the basic strains upon Liberalism caused by political and industrial crisis. Liberalism was, and is, ultimately an ideology of conscience. It was the 1914—18 War which tested that conscience rather than the earlier threats. The War also brought about an independent Labour representation in Parliament, a result of the breakdown of the Gladstone-MacDonald pact of 1903. The 'total' nature of the War brought many basic Liberal ideals into question as Robert Blake rightly states. It also led to the leadership of Asquith being challenged first with the creation of a more broadly based coalition in May 1915, and then being superseded following a split with Lloyd George in December 1916. Coalition was both a disguised concession to the Conservatives and, as Simon had said in 1914, 'the grave of Liberalism'. For the Liberal Party it meant a rift, never to be really healed, between Asquithian and Coalition Liberals. Wilson's allegory of the 'rampant omnibus' is therefore a valid one. The War may have been the bus, but was Lloyd George the driver?

The 1918 'Coupon' election returned the Coalition to power by a landslide. Yet, as Beatrice Webb saw, the victory of Lloyd George should not divert attention from the poor performance of the Asquithian Liberals, the vulnerability of many of the Coalition Liberals with their seats in industrial working-class areas to Labour advance and the 22.2 per cent of the total vote received by the Labour Party. 'Fusion' between the Coalition Liberals and Conservatives seemed possible in 1919 or 1920 — the creation of a 'centre' party to counter the reactionary Right and the revolutionary Left — but Lloyd George did not grasp this opportunity and by 1921 it was too late.

The policies of the Coalition government, especially the alleged sale of honours by Lloyd George, the Irish treaties of 1920 and 1921, the failures of the international conferences at Cannes and Genoa, and the Chanak incident of 1922 exacerbated backbench Conservative support. That dissatisfaction came to a head in October 1922 with Austen Chamberlain and Stanley Baldwin arguing the cases for and against continuing the Coalition. Baldwin's victory and the fall of the Coalition led to Lloyd George and his Liberals being without positive programmes. Lloyd George had become an electoral liability the Conservative Party could do without.

The disastrous 1922 election was followed by fusion between the two wings of the Liberal Party and they revived in the 1923 election. But this was a short-lived triumph and in the 1924 election they slumped to 40 MPs, with only 17.6 per cent of the total vote. Their decline after 1924 can be seen in the electoral statistics.

Where did Liberal support go to? The divisions within the party certainly did not help its electoral appeal. Neither did the fact that, as the Marquess of Lothian wrote in 1935, Liberal ideals were no longer as applicable to the problems of the twentieth century as they had been in earlier times. In fact both Labour and Conservative parties benefited from Liberal decline. Given that Conservative governments effectively ruled Britain for the whole of the 1918–39 period, except for 1922–3 and 1929–31, it perhaps helped the Right rather than the Left. Above all, there was the logic of the British political system which favoured a dominant two-party rather than a multi-party governmental structure.

By 1922 the Liberal Party had been relegated to the position of a minor party. It did not accept that effective policies were needed for dealing with the economic and social problems created by the First World War, and that moralistic liberal ideals were not enough. Little has changed!

Further Reading

There are two useful surveys of the Liberal Party in the twentieth century:

C. Cook, *A Short History of the Liberal Party 1900–1976* (Macmillan, 1976), a short, readable study; very useful for sixth-formers.

R. Douglas, *The History of the Liberal Party 1895–1970* (London, 1971), very sympathetic to the party but still useful.

For the Liberal Party in the years 1914–39 the following are useful:

T. Wilson, *The Downfall of the Liberal Party 1914–1935* (Fontana, 1967), which emphasises the importance of the First World War. Essential reading.

A. J. P. Taylor, *Politics in Wartime* (London, 1964) a readable and stimulating account of the 1914–18 period.

A. J. P. Taylor (ed.), *Lloyd George: Twelve Studies* (London, 1971): see especially K. Morgan on the Coalition Liberal Party.

* K. O. Morgan, *Consensus and Disunity: the Lloyd George Coalition*

Government 1918–1922 (Oxford, 1980), the definitive study of the policies and politics of this period.

* M. Kinnear, *The Fall of Lloyd George: the Political Crisis of 1922* (Macmillan, 1973)
* G. Peele and C. Cook (eds), *The Politics of Reappraisal, 1918–1939* (Macmillan, 1975), essays with an especially useful contribution by J. Campbell on Liberalism.
* C. Cook, *The Age of Alignment: Electoral Politics in Britain 1922–1929* (Macmillan, 1975), the most up-to-date analysis of the electoral changes in this period.

J. Stevenson and C. Cook, *The Slump—society and politics during the Depression* (Cape, 1977), the only real study of the Liberals in the thirties.

There are several useful autobiographies and biographies:

R. Jenkins, *Asquith* (London, 1964)

S. E. Koss, *Asquith* (London, 1976), the most recent biography, excellent reading.

* F. Owen, *Tempestuous Journey: Lloyd George, his life and times* (London, 1954), a partisan account written by a friend of the subject.

P. Rowland, *Lloyd George* (London, 1976), perhaps the best starting point until the definitive biography is written.

* Viscount Samuel, *Memoirs* (London, 1945), useful material on the late twenties and thirties.

1 A Prophetic Statement!

The British general election of 1918 seems to be curiously analogous to the German general election of 1871. Lloyd George, like Bismarck, appealed to an enormously enlarged electorate, after a dramatic national victory, for unconditional support – for a Parliament without an
5 organised opposition. In both cases the most powerful party prior to the war had been a Liberal Party which, during the war, had patriotically supported the war. In both cases there had been a small Socialist minority that had opposed the war. Bismarck's elections swept away the national Liberal Party and started a Social-Democratic Party on a career which
10 ended in its becoming, in the course of thirty or forty years, the most powerful political party in the German Empire. The Parliamentary revolution in Great Britain has been far more complete. The Liberal Party which had for years governed the Empire has been reduced to an insignificant fraction with all its leaders without exception at the bottom
15 of the poll. . . . Lloyd George with his conservative phalanx is apparently in complete command of the situation; as the only alternative Government there stands the Labour Party with its completely Socialist programme and its utopia of the equalitarian state.

> Beatrice Webb, *Diaries 1912–1924*, ed. Margaret Cole, London School of Economics, 1952, p. 141

Questions

a (i) Who was Bismarck (line 2) and what is the significance of the reference to him?

* (ii) What was the 'Social-Democratic Party' (line 9) and what part did it play in the politics of Germany in the years 1870 to 1918?

(iii) Who were 'the leaders' (line 14) of the Liberal Party in 1918 and why did they do so badly in the General Election?

* b Who was Beatrice Webb and what part did she play in the politics of the inter-war period?

c What relationship does Beatrice Webb see between war and Liberal parties? How valid do you think her assertion is?

* d Why did war place a strain upon Liberal ideology?

e To Beatrice Webb there was no alternative to 'Lloyd George with his conservative phalanx' or the Labour Party. The 1918 General Election saw the effective end of the Liberal Party's hopes as a possible governing party. Discuss.

2   Conservative Viewpoints – the End of Coalition in 1922

Mr Austen Chamberlain speaking. . . . I have asked you to meet at this moment because it is a moment fraught with grave issues for our party and for our country. . . . For months past the task of Government has been increasingly difficult, and the strain placed upon your leaders has
5 been almost indefinitely increased by the failure of unanimity of support from the party behind them. . . . There often comes a moment in the lives of parties and of Governments when they must take a critical decision. Either they must hang on and go steadily downhill more and more discredited to eventual disaster, or they take a bolder resolve and
10 they seek from those who put them in their position a renewal of the mandate that they hold. . . .

The real issue is not between Liberals and Conservatives. It is not between the old Liberal policy and the old Conservative policy. It is between those who stand for individual freedom and those who are for
15 the socialisation of the State; those who stand for free industry and those who stand for nationalization, with all its controls and all its inefficiencies. And it is at this moment . . . I am bidden to give notice to quit to the allies with whom I have worked.

. . . To us it appears that this is not the moment to break with old
20 friends, and scatter the forces which can be united in the defence of a cause which is common to us all. . . .

Mr Stanley Baldwin. . . . The Prime Minister . . . is a dynamic force, and it is from that very fact that our troubles, in my opinion arise. A dynamic force is a very terrible thing; it may crush you, but it is not
25 necessarily right.

It is owing to that dynamic force, and that remarkable personality, that

the Liberal Party, to which he formerly belonged, has been smashed to
pieces; and it is my firm conviction that, in time, the same thing will
happen to our party. . . . We have already seen, during our association
30 with him in the last four years, a section of our party hopelessly alienated
I think that if the present association is continued . . . the process must go
on inevitably until the old Conservative Party is smashed to atoms and
lost in ruins. . . .

> Report of a meeting of Conservative MPs at the Carlton Club on
> 19 October 1922; in G. Le May *British Government 1914–1953*
> *Select Documents*, Methuen, 1955, pp. 357–9

Questions

a   (i) Who were Austen Chamberlain (line 1) and Stanley Baldwin (line
22) and what part did they play in the politics of the 1918–22 period?
(ii) What were 'the grave issues' which faced the country in 1922
(line 2)?
(iii) What do 'the mandate' (line 11) and 'nationalization' (line 16)
mean?
(iv) What 'section' of the Conservative Party had been 'hopelessly
alienated' (line 30) by Lloyd George's policies?
b   Why did Chamberlain speak for continuing the Coalition and why
did Baldwin oppose it?
c   Was Baldwin correct when he argued that Lloyd George smashed the
Liberal Party to pieces?
* d   What policies did Lloyd George adopt to deal with the aftermath of
war between 1918 and 1922? How successful were they?
* e   Austen Chamberlain's belief that the 'real issue is not between Liberals
and Conservatives . . . [but] between those who stand for individual
freedom and those who are for the socialisation of the State . . .' can
help to explain why the Liberals declined as an electoral force after
1922. In British politics there was no place for two parties of the
Right or two parties of the Left. This was the Liberal dilemma
Discuss.

3 The Liberal Party in Decline – a View from Within, 1935

. . . The essential characteristic of a party is that it must have a soul, a
body of principles and emotions, vague but powerful with great masses
of people, as well as a specific policy for the immediate problems of the
hour. Toryism appeals to the instinct for conserving the tradition of the
5   past; it prefers experience to theory and appeals to those who have had
experience in practical administrative life in business and government; it
has the immense 'interest' of property and social privilege almost solidly
behind it as a source of funds and influence. The Labour Party now
includes the great mass of those who are most discontented with their

10   social or economic status; it is the party of the future; it proclaims that
Socialism is the central issue of the century as democracy was of the last,
and individual rights of earlier times, and has a vague, and largely
unpractical programme of reform; it has behind it the 'interest' of the
Trade Unions and the co-operative movement reinforced by a steadily
15   growing body of young intellectual Socialists. The Liberal Party suffers
from the fact that most of the 'causes' for which it fought – suffrage,
social reform, individual liberty, the supremacy of the House of
Commons, are already achieved. . . . There are millions of people who
still call themselves Liberal and reflect its attitude to public affairs, who are
20   not attached either to the Conservative or the Labour party, but who
seem unable to form a government and partly because they feel that what
they care about is safe under Baldwin. So they either vote 'national' or
abstain.

    I am quite sure that it is not possible to create a new party today – other
25   than the Fascist or Communist parties who may be created by events. The
practical choice is between letting the Liberal Party die and encouraging
liberally-minded people to join the other two parties in order to liberalise
them both and compel them both to be faithful to essential liberal
tradition. . . .

30   My own view is that the right course for the time being is to keep alive
the Liberal Party, until we can see more clearly the development of the
new Parliament and the domestic and international circumstances with
which it will have to deal.

Letter from the Marquess of Lothian to Lloyd George, 25
November 1935, in J. R. M. Butler, *Lord Lothian*, Macmillan,
1960, pp. 172–4. Reprinted by permission of the Twelfth
Marquess of Lothian.

Questions

(i) What was 'the immense 'interest' of property and social
privilege . . . ' (line 7) which lay behind the Conservative Party?
How influential was it?

(ii) Explain the meaning of lines 10–11. How valid an assertion is
this?

(iii) Why did the Liberals 'either vote "national" or abstain' (lines
22–3)?

b   How does the Marquess of Lothian define a political party? Do you
think his definition is correct?

c   What does he see as the appeal of both the Conservative and Labour
parties to the electorate? What were the weaknesses of the Liberal
party?

* d   The 1935 General Election was a disaster for the Liberal Party. If, as
Lothian stated 'there are millions of people who still call themselves
Liberal', why did this occur?

* e   By the 1930s the Liberal Party had been destroyed by the logic of the
two-party system of British politics. Discuss.

4   The Statistics of Decline

I General election results 1910−35

1910 *(2−19 December)*	Total votes	MPs elected	Candidates	% of total vote
Conservative	2 420 566	272	550	46.3
Liberal	2 295 888	272	467	43.9
Labour	371 772	42	56	7.1
Others	8 768	—	11	0.2
Irish Nationalist	131 375	84	106	2.5
Elec. 7 709 981	5 228 369	670	1190	100.0
Turnout 81.1%				

The remaining elections were fought with an electorate created by the 1918 Representation of the Peoples Act; and after 1928 all women over 21 could vote.

1918 *(14 December)*				
Coalition Unionist	3 504 198	335	374	32.6
Coalition Liberal	1 455 640	133	158	13.5
Coalition Labour	161 521	10	18	1.5
(Coalition)	(5 121 359)	(478)	(550)	(47.6)
Conservative	370 375	23	37	3.4
Irish Unionist	292 722	25	38	2.7
Liberal	1 298 808	28	253	12.1
Labour	2 385 472	63	388	22.2
Irish Nationalist	238 477	7	60	2.2
Sinn Fein	486 867	73	102	4.5
Others	572 503	10	197	5.3
Elec. 21 392 322	10 766 583	707	1625	100.0
Turnout 58.9%				

1922 *(15 November)*				
Conservative	5 500 382	345	483	38.2
Coalition Liberal	1 672 240	60	162	11.6
Liberal	2 516 287	56	328	17.5
Labour	4 241 383	142	411	29.5
Others	462 340	12	59	3.2
Elec. 21 127 663	14 393 632	615	1443	100.0
Turnout 71.3%				

1923 *(6 December)*				
Conservative	5 538 824	258	540	38.1
Liberal	4 311 147	159	453	29.6
Labour	4 438 508	191	422	30.5
Others	260 042	7	31	1.8
Elec. 21 281 232	14 548 521	615	1446	100.0
Turnout 70.8%				

1924 *(29 October)*				
Conservative	8 039 598	419	552	48.3
Liberal	2 308 510	40	340	17.6
Labour	5 489 077	151	512	33.0

Communist	55 346	1	8	0.3
Others	126 511	4	16	0.8
Elec. 21 731 320	16 639 279	615	1428	100.0
Turnout 76.6%				

1929 *(30 May)*

Conservative	8 656 473	260	590	38.2
Liberal	5 308 510	59	513	23.4
Labour	8 389 512	288	571	37.1
Communist	50 614	—	25	0.3
Others	243 266	8	31	1.0
Elec. 28 850 870	22 648 375	615	1730	100.0
Turnout 76.1%				

1931 *(27 October)*

Conservative	11 978 745	473	523	55.2
National Labour	341 370	13	20	1.6
Liberal National	809 302	35	41	3.7
Liberal (Samuelites)	1 403 102	33	112	6.5
(National Govt)	(14 532 509)	(554)	(969)	(67.0)
LG Liberal	106 106	4	7	0.5
Labour	6 649 630	52	515	30.6
Communist	74 824	—	26	0.3
New Party	36 377	—	24	0.2
Others	256 917	5	24	1.2
Elec. 29 960 071	21 656 373	615	1292	100.0
Turnout 76.3%				

1935 *(14 November)*

Conservative	11 810 158	432	585	53.7
Liberal	1 422 116	21	161	6.4
Labour	8 325 491	154	552	37.9
ILP	139 577	4	17	0.7
Communist	27 117	1	2	0.1
Others	272 595	4	31	1.2
Elec. 31 379 050	21 997 054	615	1348	100.0
Turnout 71.2%				

II Liberals and General Elections 1918–35

1918 Election
    Liberal *(Asquith)* elected   28
       with Coupon   8
       without Coupon   20

    Coalition Liberals *elected*   133
       with Coupon   123
       without Coupon   10
    Total Liberals *elected in 1918:*   161

1922 Election
    Liberal *(Asquith)* elected   56
      Seats held   13

Seats gained

from Conservative	31
from Coalition Liberals	10
from Labour	1
from Independent	1
Total gains	*43*

Seats lost

to Conservative	3
to Coalition Liberals	2
to Labour	9
Total losses	*14*

Coalition Liberals elected	*60*
Seats held	*57*

Seats gained

from Liberals	2
from Labour	1
Total gains	*3*

Seats lost

to Conservatives	31
to Independent Liberals	10
to Labour	39
to Independent	1
Total losses	*81*

Total Liberals elected in 1922:	*116*

1923 Election

Seats held	*77*

Seats gained

from Conservatives	68
from Labour	13
from Independent	1
Total gains	*82*

Seats lost

to Conservatives	16
to Labour	23
to Independent	2
Total losses	*41*
Total Liberals elected 1923:	*159*

1924 Election

Seats held	*31*

Seats gained

from Labour	8
from Independent	1
Total gains	*9*

Seats lost

to Conservatives	107
to Labour	16
to Communist	1
Total losses	*124*
Total Liberals elected 1924:	*40*

1929 Election
Seats held   24

Seats gained

  from Conservatives   33

  from Labour   2

Total gains   35

Seats lost

  to Labour   17

  to Independent   2

Total losses   19

Total Liberals elected 1929:   59

1931 Election
Seats held   46

Seats gained: from Labour   26

Total gains   26

Seats lost: to Conservatives   13

Total losses   13

Samuel Liberals elected   33

Lloyd George Liberals elected   4

Liberal Nationals elected   35

Total Liberals elected 1931:   72

1935 Election
Samuel Liberals elected   17

Seats held   14

Seats gained:

  from Conservatives   3

Total gains   3

Seats lost

  to Conservatives   4

  to Simonite Liberals   1

  to MacDonald Labour   1

  to Labour   11

Total losses   17

Lloyd George Liberals elected   4

Seats held   4

Simonite Liberals elected   33

Seats held   30

Seats gained

  from Conservative   2

  from Liberals   1

Total gains   3

Seats lost

  to Conservatives   1

  to Labour   6

Total losses   7

Total Liberals elected 1935 (excluding Simonites who voted with the National Government):   21

Sources: section I: D. Butler and A. Sloman *British Political Facts 1900–1975,* Macmillan, 4th edn 1975, pp. 182–4, 187–8; section II: based on appendix I in T. Wilson *The Downfall of the Liberal Party 1914–1935,* Collins, 1966, pp. 422–5

Questions

a How can the historian show this statistical material in a more manageable form?

b What information can be obtained from this material about the fragmented character of the Liberal Party between 1928 and 1935?

c What conclusions can the historian draw from this material about the loss of support for the Liberal Party? Did this support go to the Conservative Party or to the Labour Party?

* d It is ironic that the Liberal Party, which had fought for the introduction of a more democractic franchise, should have been destroyed by it. Comment.

* e An understanding of the techniques of the psephologist is essential to the historian of post-1918 Britain. Do you agree?

5 War and Peace – the Liberal Dilemma

The war was in some respects a boon politically to Asquith. The government now had the asset of a 'national' cause. 'Patriotic opposition' hamstrung the Conservatives. If the war had been over quickly . . . the Liberals would have gained ground – and one should remember that
5 many people expected the war to be just like this. But when it became obvious that the war was not only going to be long but also to be 'total'. . . the Liberals were fatally handicapped. . . . On almost every issue that came up Conservative tradition and ideology were better suited than Liberal to meet the needs of the hour. Conscription, 'defence of the
10 realm', Ireland, indeed all the necessities of a prolonged war, tended to create doubts and divisions in the Liberals. After all they were the party of liberty, and liberty is the first casualty of war. They were the party of moral conscience – and that is another casualty of war. They were the party of legalism, parliamentary forms, constitutional propriety – and
15 these also are casualties of war. Then there was sheer pacifism and its watered down version – belief in the evil of war and of any British government that waged it. True, the pro-Boers had no analogy. There were no Liberal pro-Germans. But the scruples, doubts, misgivings were there. . . .
20   Asquith was far from being an extreme representative of Liberal tendencies. . . . His whole way of thought was one that found war in its new, unprecedented and terrifying form profoundly distasteful. He thus came to symbolize to the impatient men of action everything that led to sloth and procrastination. It was inevitable that he should be elbowed out.
25 The 1915 coalition was the first step. . . . the convulsion of December 1916 and the emergence of Lloyd George cracked the Liberal party in

half. . . . With Lloyd George the Caesarism, craved before the war by some, really came into being. . . . Lloyd George was the nearest thing to a popular dictator since Cromwell and at times he treated parliament
30 almost as contemptuously. . . .

R. Blake, *The Conservative Party from Peel to Churchill*, Fontana edn 1972, pp. 195–7

Questions

a (i) What was 'total' war (line 7) and why did 'conscription' (line 9) become necessary?
(ii) Who was Asquith (line 20) and what part did he play in Liberal politics from 1908 to 1922?
(iii) Why did 'patriotic opposition' hamstring the Conservatives (lines 2–3)? Explain this in relation to the events of 1910–14.
(iv) Who were the 'pro-Boers' (line 17) and what was their significance to the Liberal Party?
(v) Explain 'the convulsion of December 1916' (lines 25–6).
b Why did both war and peace damage the electoral viability of the Liberal Party?
c Did Lloyd George destroy the Liberal Party?
* d Should Lloyd George have continued the Coalition into peacetime?
* e By 1922 the Liberal Party was bankrupt of ideas applicable to the needs of the twentieth century. Into this ideological vacuum both Conservative and Labour stole. Discuss.

6 The Liberal Decline – When Did it Begin?

It is commonly believed that the Liberal party began to fall well before 1914. . . . the Liberal party (was) doomed from the time of the Home Rule split in the 1880s; (or) from the foundation of the Independent Labour party in the 1890s, or anyway the Labour Representation
5 Committee in 1900; (or) from the election of Labour MPs in 1906; (or) from the political upheavals of the period 1910–1914 ("The Strange Death of Liberal England"). Thus to satisfy every view about when and why the Liberal party met its doom, one might as well go back to when there was a party bearing the name Liberal at all. . . .
10 The account given here is confined to the period when the Liberal party was clearly disintegrating. Such was not the case before 1914. If the party passed through troubled times between 1885 and 1905, its electoral victories between 1906 and 1910 appeared to show it fully recovered. Between 1911 and 1914 it again encountered difficulties. . . . All of these
15 are reasons for believing that the Liberal party might soon have been out of office. They do not show that it was doomed to near-extinction. . . .
To make clear the view taken here about when the Liberal party "reached the point of no return", it may be permissible to resort to allegory. The Liberal party may be compared to an individual who, after

a period of robust health and great exertion, experienced symptoms of
illness (Ireland, labour unrest, the suffragettes). Before a thorough
diagnosis could be made, he was involved in an encounter with a rampant
omnibus (the First World War), which mounted the pavement and ran
him over. After lingering painfully, he expired. A controversy has
persisted ever since as to what killed him. One medical school argues that
even without the bus he would soon have died. . . . Another school goes
further, and says that the encounter with the bus would not have proved
fatal had not the victim's health already been seriously impaired. Neither
of these views is accepted here. . . . The outbreak of the First World War
initiated a process of disintegration in the Liberal party which by 1918
had reduced it to ruins. . . .

In the half-century following 1914 the Conservatives held office
continually, with only one major interruption – the Labour government
of 1945–1951. In part this was a consequence of the decline of the left.
The left parties suffered from the loss of buoyancy and self-confidence
which followed from Britain's decline as a world power and the
experiences of the First World War, as well as from the twin phenomena
of economic growth and economic crisis which ran parallel after 1914.
The resultant urge to play safe proved largely to the advantage of the
Conservatives. So did the decline in 'idealism' . . . . Before 1914 the
Liberal and Labour parties so managed their electoral affairs that between
them they derived the maximum advantage from votes cast against the
Conservatives. After 1914 this became impossible. During the First
World War Labour became convinced – and the decrepit state of
Liberalism even by 1918 seemed to justify this conviction – that the
Liberal party would soon be extinguished altogether and that Labour
would appropriate its entire following. . . . By concentrating on de-
stroying the Liberals, Labour was ensuring its own victory "in the long
run", even though in the short run the Conservatives benefited. . . .

T. Wilson, *The Downfall of the Liberal Party 1914–1935*, Fontana
edn 1968, pp. 17–18, 20–21, 419–21

Questions

a (i) What was the 'Home Rule split in the 1880s' (lines 2–3)?
(ii) What were the 'difficulties' (line 14) which the Liberal Party
encountered between 1911 and 1914?
(iii) Explain the importance of lines 35–8.
b Examine the various dates put forward in the passage for the origins of
Liberal decline. Assess their value to the historian.
c How valid is the allegory of the individual and the rampant omnibus?
d Consider the argument that the Conservative Party benefited more
from the Liberal decline than did the Labour Party.
* e Examine in depth the vagaries of Liberal policy in the period 1914 to
1918. Is Wilson correct in his assertion that the war had reduced the
Liberal Party 'to ruins' by 1918?

Further Work

a It was the fragmentation of the Liberal Party after 1916 which led to its eventual decline. Discuss.

b Examine the various splits within the Liberal Party between 1916 and 1935. Why did they occur and what consequences did they have for the party?

c The Liberal Party has always been a party of ideas. Putting those ideas into practice has often proved hard. This may have been politically acceptable in the late nineteenth century, but not in the post-1918 period. Comment.

d Britain has a two-party political system. The Liberals failed and still fail to appreciate this. It is this, above all, which explains the decline of the Liberal Party. Do you agree?

IV In the National Interest — Conservative and Labour 1922—37

Introduction

History has not been kind to the memories of Stanley Baldwin and Ramsay MacDonald who dominated politics between 1922 and 1937. The first is still seen as the Prime Minister who thwarted both the General Strike and the marital aspirations of Edward VIII. The second is 'the great betrayer' who chose to split his party in 1931. This chapter is concerned with the motives for the actions of Ramsay MacDonald in 1931 and, in a more general sense, with the question of judgement in history.

From 1918 to 1939 British politics was dominated by the Conservative Party. Either as a dominant member of a Coalition or National government, or as a majority government, the Conservative Party retained hegemony over the system. The problems which British politicians faced in the inter-war period were primarily of an economic nature. British industry was structurally weak and uncompetitive. It is not surprising to find that two areas were of particular concern to politicians: first, the state of the staple industry, especially coal with its immense workforce; and secondly, the question of unemployment benefits.

Both Baldwin and MacDonald were enigmatic figures to contemporaries and still are today. William McElwee considers these traits. In the title of his book *Britain's Locust Years* he tries to indicate the immensity of the problem facing these men — years of plenty followed by years of shortage. How do you stop locusts eating their way across the landscape? He also raises the important question of judgement. The historian must seek 'a truer perspective' and appreciate that the problems of 1925 were different from those of 1945. Yet the picture still emerges in the national mind of Baldwin personified by his pipe and pigs and MacDonald by his vanity, ambition and betrayal. This view fails to take into account the contribution each made to his own party.

Contemporary reaction to the Cabinet split and creation of the National Government in August 1931 can be seen from two points of view in the extracts from *The Times* and the *New Statesman*. Was MacDonald's decision one of patriotism or pragmatism? Did it demonstrate the importance of the consensual nature of British politics, even in crisis?

Since the 1960s historians have begun to look at MacDonald's decision in a slightly longer perspective than just the crisis of July and August 1931. Robert Skidelsky's analysis of the second Labour government, with his emphasis on the importance of the distinction between economic radicals and economic conservatives, began the process. His neo-Keynesian approach is criticised by Ross McKibbin for the narrowness of an interpretation which is 'chiefly interesting as an explanation of the Labour Party's apparent economic conservatism' and not following up the alternative strategies open to MacDonald. McKibbin provides some useful comparative material to support those who argued for a deflationary policy. Finally the extract from Paul Adelman indicates what some of the motives behind MacDonald's actions may have been and provides some useful criticism of Skidelsky's work.

Motive is one of the primary interests of the historian. He cannot explain events without understanding the reasoning behind people actually involved or connected with them. 'The analysis of motives' is not 'relatively unimportant to the historian', as Adelman argues. To deny the importance of motive seems to imply that human action is somehow controlled by impersonal factors like economics or politics. To accept such a view could lead to the de-personification of history.

Both Baldwin and MacDonald could claim that during their periods in office they were compelled to act 'in the national interest.' The events of 1926, 1931 and 1936, and the policy of appeasement could all be justified on these grounds. Were Baldwin and MacDonald correct in their judgements? The historian's interpretation of these judgements should depend first on the evidence available, and secondly on analysis of this evidence on the basis of fair-minded, not partisan criteria. Only then can true motives be adduced.

Further Reading

Books listed and cited in chapters III and VI on the decline of the Liberals and the Depression are relevant for this chapter, too. On the Labour Party during the inter-war period the best approaches may be found in:

P. Adelman, *The Rise of the Labour Party 1880–1945* (Longman, 1972), the best starting point, with documentary material.

* K. Burgess, *The Challenge of Labour* (Croom Helm, 1980), an incisive study which explains the changing character of Labour's relationship with British society between 1850 and 1930.

C. Cook and I. Taylor (eds), *The Labour Party* (Longman, 1980), an up-to-date thematic approach to the question.

* R. I. McKibbin, *The Evolution of the Labour Party 1910–1924* (Oxford, 1974)

R. Miliband, *Parliamentary Socialism*. A study in the politics of Labour (London, 1961), a left-wing view.

H. Pelling, *A Short History of the Labour Party* (Macmillan, 3rd edn, 1968) *A History of British Trade Unionism* (Penguin, 1963) the best short introduction.

On the Conservative Party, in addition to R. Blake, see:

* J. Ramsden, *The Age of Balfour and Baldwin 1902–1940* (Longman, 1979), excellent, but not for the beginner.

D. Southgate (ed.), *The Conservative Leadership 1832–1932* (Macmillan, 1974), contains a good analysis of Baldwin as leader by the editor.

For the crisis of 1931 and the General Strike see:

R. Bassett, *Nineteen Thirty-One: Political Crisis* (London, 1958), an indispensable study, strongly pro-MacDonald.

M. Morris, *The General Strike* (Penguin, 1976), perhaps the best analysis which contains some seminal local studies.

J. Symons, *The General Strike* (Cresset Press, 1957), a good popular account with much eye-witness material.

There are now good biographies of both Baldwin and MacDonald:

G. M. Young, *Stanley Baldwin* (1952), a highly unsatisfactory official account which led to a corrective account by his son:

A. W. Baldwin, *My Father: The True Story* (1955).

K. Middlemas and J. Barnes *Baldwin* (1969), is a vast biography.

The partisan accounts of MacDonald, a consequence of 1931, were answered by the definitive study:

D. Marquand, *Ramsay MacDonald* (Cape, 1977).

It is unfortunate that there is still no good study of Baldwin's periods as prime minister, and that the second MacDonald government has not been looked at from views other than that of economic policy. The National Government from 1931 to 1937 is similarly in need of analysis.

1 The Baldwin-MacDonald Regime

It was the fate of both of these men to become, at the end of their lives, centres of the most embittered controversy. MacDonald was to die with the curses of those in whose service he had spent his life ringing in his ears for the 'great betrayal' of 1931. Baldwin's declining years were poisoned

5 by thousands of bitter, reproachful letters from those who laid all the disasters of 1940 and the sufferings of London under the bombings at the door of his political cowardice. It is possible that this witch-hunting mania, particularly in Baldwin's case, has still not died down sufficiently for the historian to penetrate to the real contribution of these men whose

10 personalities Churchill rightly saw as the dominating factors in English public life for over a decade. Most of the published memoirs still reek of contemporary prejudice, contemporary ignorance, and a partisan blindness to facts. The historian, seeking some truer perspective, must remember how different the problems of 1925 were from those of 1945;

15 and must in fairness record that both men succeeded abundantly in certain tasks for which their abilities remarkably fitted them, and failed sadly in others for which they were quite unfitted. It is also wise to remember that a democracy does on the whole get the leaders it deserves. . . .

To his colleagues and contemporaries Stanley Baldwin appeared

20 always as something of an enigma – often a maddening enigma. Certainly there was none of that simplicity of character which English-

men love to simulate and so rarely possess. For the cartoonists and the
public at large there was the bowler hat and the pipe, the Sunday walks in
Worcestershire which ended in the contemplation of his pigs; Squire
25 Baldwin, simple, straightforward, homely and above all
trustworthy. . . . Many of the accusations which have been levelled at
him were, of course, true. . . . he was indolent. . . . He did not lead
Cabinet meetings through a prepared agenda. . . . He let discussion
range until it reached a conclusion. . . . To colleagues his
30 detachment. . . was maddening. . . .

In attempting . . . to remedy the existing state of affairs, Baldwin had
thus set himself a double task. In the first place he had to lead
Conservatives to some imaginative understanding of the situation which
had called a Labour Party into being and to convince them that their
35 survival depended on finding a better practical solution to the problems
than Labour's. Secondly, he sought to convince Labour that all
Conservatives were not blood-sucking capitalists, that humanity and
idealism were not the exclusive prerogatives of left-wing
thinkers. . . . MacDonald had the same task in reverse. He had to
40 convince the nation that Labour was a responsible party, perfectly
competent to take over the government, and resolved to achieve its
programme of reforms within the framework of the constitution. He had
also to persuade Labour itself that it was in and through Parliament that
social progress could be best achieved: that the existing constitutional
45 structure was not designed to shore up capitalism and preserve privilege,
but was available to any party which could secure a democratically
elected majority.

William McElwee, *Britain's Locust Years 1918–1940*, Faber, 1962,
pp. 93–6

Questions

a   What were 'the great betrayal of 1931' (line 4) and 'the disasters of
1940' (lines 5–6)?
b   What questions of methodology does the author raise which the
historian considering Baldwin and MacDonald should bear in mind?
c   What picture of Baldwin's personality emerges from this extract?
d   What political tasks did Baldwin and MacDonald have to solve?
* e   Is it valid to talk of the period 1923–37 as the Baldwin-MacDonald
Regime?
* f   Do democracies on the whole get the leaders they deserve?

2   Journalistic Reaction in 1931

The country awakens this morning to find Mr MacDonald still Prime
Minister, with the prospect of a small Cabinet representative of all three
parties. The former Cabinet resigned yesterday afternoon, and a
statement issued last night announced that considerable progress had been

5 made towards settling the composition of its successor, which would be a
   Government of co-operation formed with the specific purposes only of
   carrying through a very large reduction in expenditure and raising 'on an
   equitable basis' the further funds required to balance the Budget. . . .
        All concerned are to be warmly congratulated on this result, so fully in
10 accord with the patriotic spirit which has inspired a week's most anxious
   negotiations. The Prime Minister and the colleagues of his own party
   who have followed him deserve in particular unqualified credit, both for
   the manner in which they took their political lives in their hands by facing
   and forcing the break-up of the late Cabinet, and for their new decision to
15 translate courage in the Cabinet into courage in the country.The
   readiness to share the responsibility—honour is perhaps the better
   word—of carrying through to the end the policy of retrenchment adds
   enormously to the prospect of its success.
        The Times, 25 August 1931

   In many respects the situation which confronted the Cabinet was like
20 that of August 1914. . . . In 1914 Mr MacDonald refused to join a War
   Cabinet: Mr Henderson accepted. Mr MacDonald was denounced as a
   traitor: Mr Henderson applauded. In leading articles in *The Times*, for
   instance, Mr MacDonald's patriotism is extolled, while Mr Henderson is
   denounced as a man who put party before country. Meanwhile, in
25 Labour circles all over the country Mr MacDonald is being denounced. . . . for betraying his party. . . . Mr MacDonald's decision to
   form a Cabinet in conjunction with the Liberals and the Tories seems to
   us a mistake, just as it would have been a mistake for him as a pacifist to
   join a War Cabinet in 1914. For he must inevitably find himself at war
30 with the whole of organised labour, and not only with organised labour,
   but with all those, in all classes, who believe that the policy of reducing
   the purchasing power of the consumer to meet a situation of over-
   production is silly economics. . . . An effort is being made to represent
   the whole issue as merely one of a 10 percent reduction in the dole and
35 refusal to cut it could only be based on cowardly subservience to the
   electorate. . . . We oppose it . . . because it is only the first step, the
   crucial beginning of a policy of reductions, disastrous, we believe for
   England and the rest of the world. . . .
        New Statesman, 29 August 1931

Questions

a (i) Explain the significance of the 'prospect of a small Cabinet
   representative of all three parties' (lines 2–3).
   (ii) What were the economic ideas contained in lines 7–8 and 17.
   (iii) What were the parallels between the situation in 1931 and that of
   August 1914 (lines 19–20)?
   (iv) Who was Mr Henderson (line 21) and what part did he play in
   the development of the Labour Party?

(v) What economic ideas are contained in lines 33−5?

(vi) What was 'the dole' (line 34)?

b What information can be obtained from these extracts about the views of these papers?

c Why did MacDonald take the decision to retrench in August 1931?

* d What role did the Press play in the politics of the inter-war period?

* e Was the formation of the National Government in 1931 'a mistake' (line 28)?

3   Towards 1931 – Skidelsky's Interpretation

Interest in the Labour Government of 1929 to 1931 has centred almost exclusively on the events leading to the formation of the National Government on 24 August 1931. . . . One unfortunate consequence of this is that it reinforces the tendency to view inter-war politics in terms of
5 a struggle between socialism and capitalism, between the Labour Party and the Rest. This was undoubtedly an important cleavage, especially of sentiment, and as such should not be underestimated. However, the real cleavage of opinion occurred not across this divide, but another; between the economic radicals and the economic conservatives. This cut right
10 across party lines. . . . The real story of the domestic politics of the inter-war period is the defeat of the economic radicals by the economic conservatives.

The issue on which this debate centred was unemployment. Unemployment of 10 per cent was endemic in the England of the nineteen-
15 twenties. It is often argued that before Keynes's General Theory (1936) governments were bound to pursue conservative, orthodox, economic policies. Yet most economists and many businessmen rejected the 'treasury view', and dissent from orthodoxy increased progressively as traditional policies failed to restore prosperity. By 1929 there existed a
20 substantial body of economic and political support for a radical unemployment policy embracing an expansionist monetary policy and a big programme of government investment. . . . Why did the Labour Party fail to utilize this dissent for the ends of a radical unemployment policy? . . .

25 The failure of the 1929 Labour Government . . . determined the politics of the following decade. Could that failure have been prevented? Usually criticism of MacDonald and his colleagues starts with their handling of the financial crisis of 1931 rather than with their omissions over the previous two years. But whereas between 1929 and 1931 there
30 were plenty of effective choices open to Government, in 1931 itself there was virtual unanimity on the need to defend the gold standard . . . MacDonald broke with his colleagues not over policy but over primary loyalty. As Prime Minister he considered his first duty was to the 'national interest' as it was almost universally conceived; the
35 Labour Party saw its first duty to its own people. . . . The real criticism of MacDonald is not that he formed the National Government, but that

under his leadership the Labour Government had drifted into a position
which left it so little choice. . . . the Government rejected Conservative
protection, the Liberal national development loan, the Keynesian and
40   Mosleyite amalgams of both, preferring instead the advice of the least
progressive sections of the 'economic establishment'.

　　　　　R. Skidelsky *Politicians and the Slump: the Labour Government of*
　　　　　1929–1931, Penguin, 1970, pp. 11–12, 425–6

Questions

a   (i) Who were 'the economic radicals and the economic
　　　conservatives' (lines 9–12)?
　　　(ii) What was 'Keynes's General Theory' (line 15) and why has it
　　　been so influential?
　　　(iii) What were 'the treasury view' (line 18) and 'the gold standard'
　　　(lines 31–2)?
　　　(iv) In what ways would 'an expansionist monetary policy and a big
　　　programme of government investment' (lines 21–2) have led to a
　　　radical unemployment policy?
b   Skidelsky sees the 1929–31 period in terms of the relationship
　　　between radical and conservative economists. Discuss.
c   Skidelsky both attacks and defends MacDonald. How?
d   Primary loyalty rather than policy. Is this the key to understanding
　　　MacDonald's decision in August 1931?
*   *e*   Was the crisis of 1931 purely economic?

4   Economic Policy 1929–31

Until the last ten years or so the second Labour Government was
conventionally seen in terms of its fall. It came to office in 1929 after an
election which gave no party a majority, and which left it dependent on
the support of the Liberals. It fell in August 1931 when its members were
5   unable to agree upon a programme of budgetary economies that would
satisfy both the Conservative and Liberal parties. . . . The 'desertion' of
MacDonald caused great bitterness and generated a partisan history
usually designed to justify the behaviour of one side or the other in the
debacle. The level of strictly economic content was usually not high. But
10   with release of public and private records on the one hand, and with the
general acceptance of a developed Keynesianism on the other, a newer
school has sought only to explain why the Labour government did not
adopt economic policies which might appear to have been obviously the
right ones. Why did it not, for example, attempt to reverse economic
15   contraction by a programme of public works financed by budget deficits,
or by tax-cuts, or–a policy less untypical of a socialist party–by a
redistribution of income that might have raised demand? Why was the
government apparently so inflexibly attached to existing monetary
policies?
20   　　　The most sustained and stimulating 'neo-Keynesian' analysis of the

second MacDonald ministry is Dr Robert Skidelsky's *Politicians and the Slump*. This book is chiefly interesting as an explanation of the Labour Party's apparent economic conservatism, but he does not doubt that an alternative was readily at hand. 'The absence of developed Keynesian theory', he writes

was not a decisive barrier to the adoption of what might loosely be termed Keynesian economics, as is proved by the experience of the United States, Germany, France and Sweden which in the 1930s all attempted, with varying success, to promote economic recovery through deficit budgeting. In Sweden this was done especially effectively by a democratic Labour Government operating a normal parliamentary system.

Dr Skidelsky implies here two propositions: that alternative policies towards the economic depression were wilfully ignored by the Labour government, and that international comparison shows that these policies were more or less effective ones. . . .

Two of the assumptions upon which all British governments worked were true enough to inhibit innovation here even more than in the United States or Sweden. The 1929 Labour government assumed, first, that the problems of the British economy were partly structural; and secondly, that Britain's place in the international economy almost uniquely influenced its monetary policies. These assumptions were related: structural weakness (so the argument went) led to falling exports and payments difficulties, which in turn exacerbated Britain's 'international' problems. On the other hand, the requirements of the City led to monetary policies that made internal reconstruction difficult.

Both these propositions were powerful impediments to economic unorthodoxy. It was unquestionable that British industry had failed in the post-war world, partly because it was concentrated in staples . . . producing goods that people did not want . . . .

The practicable alternatives open to the Labour government were not drift or reflation, but drift or deflation. Until the crisis of July-August 1931, Britain alone of the major countries seriously affected by the depression refused to follow deflationary policies. Her relatively generous social services were not only maintained but somewhat increased in scope; despite the shrinking of the tax-base, government expenditure continued to rise; no serious attempt was made to balance the budget. . . .

The second Labour government collapsed in August 1931 when the pressure to abandon drift and adopt deflation became too strong. Two movements came together: the pressure to solve Britain's internal budgetary problems by deflation reached its peak when the May report was published on 31st July — at the same time as the European liquidity crisis reached London and immediately called into question the exchange rate of the pound. The budgetary crisis and the exchange crisis were originally distinct phenomena, but throughout August 1931 they played upon each other.

R. McKibbin 'The Economic Policy of the Second Labour Government 1929-1931', *Past and Present*, volume 68, August 1975, pp. 95–6, 102–3, 114–15

Questions

* *a* Should the historian be concerned with why particular policies were not adopted?
  b What alternative strategies does McKibbin consider were open to the Labour government between 1929 and 1931?
  c What are the main points from Skidelsky's book which the author highlights in his article?
  d What were 'the two assumptions' (line 36) which inhibited innovation by British governments?
* *e* The failure of economic orthodoxy is the key to understanding 1931. Do you agree?
  f MacDonald was adrift in an economic sea over which he had no control. The choice of a conservative economic solution reflects either an awareness of what the public wanted or a faint heart. Discuss.

5   MacDonald's Motivation

How are we to explain MacDonald's conduct? It is probably true that, as his critics aver, he was vain, ambitious, and increasingly out of touch with rank-and-file sentiment within the party, and this explains his inability to appreciate the depth of feeling over the ten per cent cut. But there is no
5 real evidence, as Bassett has shown, that MacDonald was either in sympathy with or had been planning to become leader of a 'National Government' before the events of August 1931 thrust the role upon him. For a generation after this crisis Ramsay MacDonald was branded as a traitor to the Labour movement; but most impartial historians now agree
10 with the spirit of Bassett's remark that 'he was moved primarily by his sense of duty', even though we need not accept his further implication that what was good for MacDonald was also good for the Labour Party. What gave weight to MacDonald's actions too was his belief that his leadership of the National Government would be temporary: as he
15 stressed to his colleagues at that last fateful Cabinet meeting, it was to deal with an extraordinary crisis only, and, as had happened after 1918, he would return to the fold later on to lead a reunited party. For his Labour colleagues, as MacDonald himself seems to have accepted, the position was different: for them the primary issue was one of party loyalty and not
20 the question of the unemployment cuts (over which the gap between the two groups was very narrow), or a vague 'national interest' over whose meaning no one could agree. After all, a majority of the Cabinet had supported all of the cuts, and even the minority must have accepted that they would in any case be imposed by the next Conservative/Liberal
25 government. For most Labour ministers the major question was, therefore, as Professor Medlicott has emphasised (in *Contemporary England 1914–64*), how to avoid a major split within the party, and on this issue a majority preferred to resign together rather than follow the Prime Minister into the National Government and accept a major breach in the
30 Cabinet and the party.

This analysis of motives, though fascinating to the psychologist, is now relatively unimportant to the historian: the real question to be asked about MacDonald's behaviour in August 1931, Skidelsky suggests, is how 'under his leadership the Labour Government had drifted into a
35 position which left it so little choice'. The answer to this question, he believes, lies in the economic failures of the Labour Government before the crisis in the summer of 1931; and their failures were a necessary consequence of the 'Utopian ethic' to which the party was committed.

The Labour Party's commitment to a nebulous Socialism [Skidelsky writes]
40 made it regard the work of the 'economic radicals' such as Keynes as mere 'tinkering', when in fact it was they who were providing the real choice. It was the failure of the Labour Party to recognise that this was the choice that doomed it to failure and sterility in this crucial period.

In a recent article ('1929–1931 Revisited', *Society for the Study of*
45 *Labour History Bulletin*, no.21, Autumn 1970) Skidelsky has gone further, and argued that the Labour Party's failure was a failure not so much of socialism itself, but of Victorian liberalism, the parent ideology from which British socialism sprang and which, in its economic aspect at least, had persisted virtually unchallenged well into the twentieth century.
50 Skidelsky's main thesis, and its later refinement, both seem to exaggerate the influence of ideas, or their absence, as an explanation of economic and political events. It may perhaps be suggested that the second Labour Government's economic failures have rather deeper roots than Skidelsky suggests. . . . On 21 September 1931 . . . Britain abandoned the gold
55 standard. Bank rate was then raised to six per cent, and for the moment this brought to an end the long-drawn-out financial crisis. As Taylor comments (in *English History 1914–1945*): 'A few days before, a managed economy had seemed as wicked as family planning. Now, like contraception, it became a commonplace. This was the end of an age'.

P. Adelman, *The Rise of the Labour Party 1880–1945*, Longman, 1972, pp. 70–72

Questions

a (i) What are 'the gold standard', 'Bank rate' (lines 54–5) and 'a managed economy' (lines 57–8)?
(ii) What was 'the ten per cent cut' (line 4)?
(iii) Explain the reference to 1918 (line 16).
(iv) Explain how it was that 'Victorian liberalism' was 'the parent ideology from which British socialism sprang' (lines 47–8).
b What information about MacDonald's motives in 1931 can be adduced from this passage?
c In what ways did MacDonald's and his ministers' perceptions of the possible results of the crisis differ?
d What are Skidelsky's views on the character of the crisis of 1931 and in what ways has he modified his original contentions?
e In what ways may Skidelsky's views be criticised?

* *f* 'Analysis of motives, though fascinating to the psychologist, is now relatively unimportant to the historian' (lines 31–2). Do you accept this as a basis for historical analysis either in the case of MacDonald or in a more general sense?

Further Work

a Why did Baldwin succeed in 1926 and MacDonald fail in 1931?

b The Conservative Party, either as a majority government or as part of a Coalition or National government, dominated inter-war politics. Why?

c MacDonald, like Peel in 1846, Gladstone in 1886 and Lloyd George in 1916, put country above party. Why did contemporaries find this so difficult to understand?

d Why did the Labour Party hold office for such a short time in the inter-war period?

e Classical or Keynesian economics? Was the choice between them the key issue of politics between 1924 and 1937?

f How can the historian judge people and their actions?

g How has MacDonald's decision in 1931 coloured the attitude of Labour politicians since 1945?

V   Winston Churchill: from Defeat into Victory?

Introduction

To most of those who lived in Britain during the first half of the twentieth century the greatest national personality was Winston Churchill, especially after his wartime premiership, 1940–45. Indeed, for years after he retired from active politics it was almost impossible to consider his whole career objectively, and many books on him, like Guedalla's, were pure hagiography, in which his exclusion from office between 1929 and 1939 and the ignoring of his warnings on the threat from Fascism and Nazism were apparently caused purely by the stupidity and jealousy of inter-war politicians. Subsequently, historians like Robert Rhodes James and Martin Gilbert have examined in detail Churchill's reputation between the wars as a failed politician, who had been guilty of misjudgement so many times, from Tonypandy in 1910 through the early years of the First World War as First Lord of the Admiralty, as the minister responsible for the 'ten-year rule' to the mediocre Chancellor lambasted by J. M. Keynes. In this light the events of the 1930s – India, the Abdication Crisis, his attacks on Baldwin – were further examples to contemporaries of how Churchill was reliving the unfulfilled career of his father, Lord Randolph, whose political life ended abruptly in 1886 at the age of 37.

Churchill's early life reveals many aspects of his political ideas, including his thirst for action. Even in 1944 at the age of 70 he was only dissuaded by King George VI from landing on the Normandy beaches a few days after D-Day! His sense of history, interestingly revealed in his many history books, was very strong and 'whiggish', in which the genius of the English-speaking peoples had won a great Empire and achieved a near-perfect system of government. This limited conception of England's history blinded Churchill to many problems, like the demand for Indian self-government but, as J. H. Plumb said, was his great strength in the dark years of 1940–41. As Stanley Baldwin, his opponent of the 1930s, had written of Lloyd George, 'war smelted out all the base metal from him.'

Churchill was unique among the great twentieth-century statesmen in consciously preparing during the Second World War his account of the war and of his role within it. He realised the importance of being first in the field with *The Gathering Storm* (1948) and it will take a long time before the public image of the war can be pulled away from the mould provided by Churchill.

To some, the historian-biographer destroying aspects of the Churchill legend is an iconoclast, but the test of time is unlikely to change materially the greatest years of Churchill's life from 1940 to 1945 during which he uplifted the people of Britain in one of the greatest crises of their history.

Further Reading

V. Bonham Carter, *Winston Churchill As I Knew Him* (Eyre & Spottiswoode and Collins, 1965), a personal memoir by Asquith's daughter of the years to 1916 in which she knew him closely.

W. S. Churchill, *My Early Life* (Collins, 1930), several of the themes of Churchill's later life have their origin in these years and can be easily recognised here.

W. S. Churchill, *The World Crisis* (Thornton Butterworth, 1923–7; abridged edition, 1931), Churchill's account of the First World War, very good on descriptions of war, and wittily described by A. J. Balfour as 'brilliant autobiography disguised as a history of the universe.'

H. Pelling, *Winston Churchill* (Macmillan, 1974), a good critical book, more manageable for the whole of Churchill's life than Gilbert's volumes.

A. J. P. Taylor *et al.*, *Churchill: Four Faces and the Man* (Allen Lane/Penguin, 1969), a fascinating, often iconoclastic but always stimulating collection of five essays, including Taylor on 'The Statesman', R. R. James on 'The Politician' and J. H. Plumb on 'The Historian'.

I Walking with Destiny

Twilight War ended with Hitler's assault on Norway. . . . We were still a party Government, under a Prime Minister from whom the Opposition was bitterly estranged, and without the ardent and positive help of the trade union movement. . . . The stroke of catastrophe and the spur of peril were needed to call forth the dormant might of the British nation. . . .

The many disappointments and disasters of the brief campaign in Norway caused profound perturbation at home, and the currents of passion mounted even in the breasts of some of those who had been most slothful and purblind in the years before the war. The Opposition asked for a debate on the war situation. . . . One speaker after another from both sides of the House attacked the Government, and especially its chief, with unusual bitterness and vehemence. . . . From the benches behind the Government Mr Amery quoted, amid ringing cheers, Cromwell's imperious words to the Long Parliament: 'You have sat too long here for any good you have been doing. . . . In the name of God, go!' . . .

I had volunteered to wind up the debate. . . . I did this with good heart

when I thought of [the Labour Opposition's] mistakes and dangerous
pacifism in former years and how only four months before the outbreak
20   of the war they had voted solidly against conscription. . . . The
Government had a majority of 81, but over 30 Conservatives voted with
the Labour and Liberal Oppositions, and a further 60 abstained. . . .

The morning of the 10th of May dawned, and with it came
tremendous news. . . . The Germans had struck their long-awaited
25   blow. . . . The whole movement of the German Army upon the
invasion of the Low Countries and of France had begun. . . .

At eleven o'clock I was . . . summoned to Downing Street
by   the   Prime   Minister.   There . . . I   found   Lord   Halifax.
[Chamberlain] . . . told us that he was satisfied that it was beyond his
30   power to form a National Government. The response . . . from the
Labour leaders left him in no doubt of this. The question therefore was
whom he should advise the King to send for. . . .

Presently a message arrived summoning me to the Palace at six
o'clock. . . .

35   His Majesty received me most graciously and bade me sit down. He
looked at me searchingly and quizzically for some moments, and then
said, 'I suppose you don't know why I have sent for you?' Adopting his
mood, I replied, 'Sir, I simply couldn't imagine why.' He laughed and
said, 'I want to ask you to form a Government.' I said I would certainly do
40   so. . . .

Thus . . . at the outset of this mighty battle, I acquired the chief power
in the State, which . . . I wielded in ever-growing measure for five years
and three months of world war, at the end of which time, all our enemies
having surrendered unconditionally or being about to do so, I was
45   immediately dismissed by the British electorate from all further conduct
of their affairs. . . .

At last I had the authority to give directions over the whole scene. I felt
as if I were walking with destiny, and that all my past life had been but a
preparation for this hour and for this trial. Ten years in the political
50   wilderness had freed me from ordinary party antagonisms. My warnings
over the last six years had been so numerous, so detailed, and were now so
terribly vindicated, that no one could gainsay me. . . .

W. S. Churchill, *The Gathering Storm*, Cassell, 1948 [Penguin
edn 1960], pp. 572–3, 582–5, 587–9.

Questions

a   Identify 'Twilight War' (line 1); 'the Opposition' (line 2) and
Churchill's own office at this time.

b   Who and what were the speakers in the Commons debate attacking?
Why did Churchill find some of their attitudes ironic?

c   What 'warnings over the last six years' (lines 50–1) had Churchill
given? Why had they been ignored?

d   Which events of 1940 were in the author's mind when he wrote of
'the stroke of catastrophe and the spur of peril' (lines 4–5)?

* e Why was the party led by Churchill defeated in 1945? Examine Churchill's attitude to his defeat, as stated in this document.
* f Examine the political events of May 1940 in which Churchill was invited by the King to form a National Government. Was he the only person suitable for that task?
  g What evidence of exaggeration and bias can be found in the passage?

2   The Hero of 1940

The Trade Unions' attempt to paralyse the community into acquiescence in their view of a just settlement was unsuccessful largely because it tried a pre-war weapon on a post-war public. An essential element in the maintenance of confidence was the continued dissemination of news.
5 Broadcasting had not yet become a universal medium; and the newspapers had practically vanished. In these circumstances there was a good deal to be said for improvising an official journal; and who was a more likely editor than Mr. Churchill? True, he had done nothing of the kind before. But his colleagues entertained a touching faith in his
10 journalistic experience, and presently he found himself in charge of the presses of the *Morning Post* with editorial control of a new daily paper named the *British Gazette*. It managed to get printed and distributed; its circulation soared; and the editor enjoyed himself immensely. Years afterwards he spoke of his delight in the spectacle of 'a great newspaper
15 office, with its machines crashing and grinding away, for it reminds me of the combination of a first-class battleship and a first-class general election'; and here he was in May, 1926, with his own editorial command to exercise in the heartening stamp and thunder of his own presses. It was a great experience; and it did good service in the controversy which called
20 it into being, although it failed to satisfy those of its readers who took a more detached view of the issues raised by the General Strike. . . .

Looking still further into the practical requirements of an unpleasant future, Mr. Churchill pleaded for a combined Ministry of Defence to co-ordinate the needs of the three Services. . . . But his clearest call was for 'a
25 large vote of credit to double our Air Force . . . and a larger vote of credit as soon as possible to redouble the Air Force.'

Obsessed with the exposed position of the country and 'our enormous Metropolis here, the greatest target in the world, 'he asked pointed questions about the furtive growth of Geman air power and stated that it
30 was already overhauling Britain's and would pass it in the course of 1936. . . .

[The Abdication Crisis] had left its mark upon his prospects. For his intervention sharply depressed the rising scale of Mr. Churchill's fortunes, and the sad transaction gave Mr. Baldwin a new lease of
35 life. . . . while Mr. Churchill's temporary eclipse, attributable to his honest advocacy of a straightforward course in circumstances of great difficulty, postponed to a more distant future his inevitable return to office. . . .

P. Guedalla, *Mr. Churchill, A Portrait*, Hodder & Stoughton, 1941, pp. 237–8, 257, 265

Questions

a What does the author tell us about Churchill's part in the General Strike? Is it a balanced account?

b What was ironic about Churchill's 'clearest call . . . for 'a large vote of credit to double our Air Force . . . ' (lines 24–5)?

c How valid is Guedalla's comment on 'Mr. Churchill's temporary eclipse . . .[which] postponed to a more distant future his inevitable return to office' (lines 35–8)?

d From these extracts what do you judge is the author's theme on Churchill between the wars?

e What significance might be attached to the year of publication of this book? Could it attempt to be an objective portrayal of its subject?

3 Reappraisal

Throughout the five years of the Conservative Government, from 1924 to 1929, there was a running undercurrent of conflict between Baldwin and Churchill. Baldwin wanted to win over the working class and to make the Labour party fully at home in the constitutional courses as a
5 preliminary to crushing them. Churchill wanted to treat Labour as an irreconcilable enemy. . . . As in other matters, the British people were in no mood for a fight. The one cause which might have injected some passion into politics was Protection. But Churchill was debarred from using this weapon against Baldwin by his own belief in Free Trade. He
10 sought some other topic which might shatter the complacent calm of the Baldwin era.

He   believed   that   he   had   found   this   topic . . . in India. . . . Churchill . . . had been for conciliation so long as it was a matter   of   generosity,   resting   on   strength.   When   the   Indian
15 nationalists . . . began to practise non-violent resistance . . . Churchill took up the challenge. He remembered the India of his youth and looked with romantic admiration on the Indian princes. India became Churchill's obsession. On this issue, he broke with Baldwin, abandoned his high position in the Conservative party, and went into solitary
20 opposition. This was a period of grave crisis. The world was ravaged by the Great Depression. There were nearly three million unemployed in Great Britain. In 1931 a National Government was formed to save the pound and instead was forced to abandon the gold standard. Abroad, the security established after the First World War crumbled. Hitler and the
25 Nazis were marching to victory in Germany. Meanwhile, Churchill, who had often shown himself a statesman of great wisdom, could only reiterate his devotion to the Indian princes and his opposition to all constitutional concession. . . .

It has puzzled later observers that Churchill was disregarded when
30 dangers and difficulties accumulated for Great Britain. Baldwin and
Ramsay MacDonald . . . have been blamed for their sloth and blindness,
and the British people have been blamed as well. . . . But the fault lay
also with Churchill himself. He lost all hold on British opinion by his
intemperate opposition over India. The British people would not respond
35 to the romantic call of Imperial glory. Rightly or wrongly, they were
committed to the cause of constitutional concession, and Churchill's
resistance seemed to them irrelevant obscurantism. He was the more
diminished because on the great economic questions of the moment he
had nothing to say. He remained silent during the interminable debates
40 over unemployment, Protection, and economic recovery. . . .
  A. J. P. Taylor, 'The Statesman' in *Churchill: Four Faces and the
  Man*, Allen Lane/Penguin 1969 [1973 edn], pp. 23–5

Questions

a What event of the 1920s was Churchill involved in, which explains
   Taylor's comment (lines 5–6)?
b What was the debate on Free Trade and Protection?
c How had 'the India of his youth' (line 16) affected Churchill's vision
   of it in the 1930s?
d Why did Taylor think that Churchill's obsession with India was a
   serious mistake?
* e In view of Churchill's Cabinet rank from 1924 to 1929, why was it
      surprising that 'on the great economic questions of the moment he
      had nothing to say' (lines 38–9)?
* f Is this a satisfactory explanation of why Churchill was so long in the
      wilderness, and his warnings consistently ignored? Does the reader
      need to investigate the extent to which Taylor's views make
      him unsympathetic towards Churchill?

4 India

. . . The rescue of India from ages of barbarism, tyranny, and intestine
war, and its slow but ceaseless forward march to civilisation constitute
upon the whole the finest achievement of our history. This work has been
done in four or five generations by the willing sacrifices of the best of our
5 race. War has been banished from India; her frontiers have been defended
against invasion from the north; famine has been gripped and
controlled. . . . Justice has been given – equal between race and race,
impartial between man and man. Science, healing or creative, has been
harnessed to the service of this immense and, by themselves, helpless
10 population. . . .
  It has been since the Great War . . . a declared object of the British
nation to aid the peoples of India to become consciously identified with
the whole process of their own elevation and advance. No limits have

been assigned within the broad constitution of the British Empire to the
15 assumption by Indians and by India of full responsible government,
except those limits – hard, physical, obvious, and moral – arising from
Time and Facts. A vast expansion of self-administering and self-
governing duties was accorded to the Indian political classes ten years ago
by the Montagu Constitution. . . .

20   It is . . . the duty of public men and of political parties to make it
plain . . . that the extension of Dominion status to India is not practicable
at the present time. . . . [It] can certainly not be attained by a community
which brands and treats sixty millions of its members, fellow human
beings . . . as 'Untouchables', whose approach is an affront and whose
25 very presence is pollution . . . [nor] while India is a prey to fierce racial
and religious dissensions and when the withdrawal of British protection
would mean the immediate resumption of mediaeval wars. . . .

    Yet we are told Indian opinion has changed so rapidly. . . . Classes,
races, creeds, opposed for centuries, are now uniting in a common desire
30 to terminate the British connection. What is the cause of this
change? . . . It is the weak-minded and defeatist tendency of our present
politics which must bear the main responsibility. . . .

    Our concessions will . . . only be used as the starting-point for new
demands by revolutionaries, while the loyal elements and the masses of
35 the people will be the more unsettled by further evidences of British
weakness. The Truth is that Gandhi-ism and all it stands for will . . . have
to be grappled with and finally crushed. It is no use trying to satisfy a tiger
by feeding him with cat's-meat. . . .

    We have no intention of casting away that most truly bright and
40 precious jewel in the crown of the King, which more than all our other
Dominions and Dependencies constitutes the glory and strength of the
British Empire. The loss of India would mark and consummate the
downfall of the British Empire. That great organism would pass at a stroke
out of life into history. From such a catastrophe there could be no
45 recovery. . . .

    It is alarming and also nauseating to see Mr. Gandhi, a seditious Middle
Temple lawyer, now posing as a fakir of a type well-known in the East,
striding half-naked up the steps of the Vice-regal palace, while he is still
organising and conducting a defiant campaign of civil disobedience, to
50 parley on equal terms with the representative of the King-Emperor. . . .

    I think it vital that the Conservative party should without delay get
itself into a strong position of resistance, and should begin to arouse public
opinion throughout the country against these most unwise and dangerous
proceedings. I intend at any rate to do my best. . . . India is no ordinary
55 question of party politics. It is one of those supreme issues which come
upon us from time to time. When they arise the men and women who
faithfully guard the life of Britain and her Empire in every rank and
employment, in every part of the country, feel the same vibration. They
felt it on August 4, 1914. They felt it in the General Strike. They feel it
60 now. . . .

W. S. Churchill, *India, Speeches and an Introduction*, Thornton
Butterworth, 1931, pp. 30–31, 34–5, 40–41, 46–7, 94–5

Questions

a   What did Churchill probably mean by 'those limits . . . arising from
Time and Facts' (lines 16–17)?

b   Identify signs of condescension to the Indians in these speeches.

c   During a Commons debate on the Government of India Bill, 1935,
Leo Amery said that all of Churchill's speeches on India were 'utterly
and entirely negative and devoid of constructive thought.' Is this true
of these extracts? Was he the only major politician who thought on
these lines?

*   d   Whom did Churchill blame for the state of affairs in India? What had
the Viceroy, Lord Irwin, recently announced?

*   e   Was Churchill misjudging public opinion in his historical parallels
(lines 59–60)?

*   f   Did Churchill cry 'Wolf!' too often on various issues in the 1930s, and
therefore lessen his impact in foreign affairs?

5   A Failure?

Let us attempt his portrait in November 1918. Behold him, then, after
eighteen years of active politics and over ten years in office. Much of the
early aggressiveness has been softened by age and experience. In manner
he remains alert, thrusting, eager or, in sharp contrast fitting his mood,
5   sombre, portentous and scowling with leaden responsibility. On the
platform or in the . . . Commons he is capable of sharp retort and vivid
repartee, yet behind all his major speeches there lie hours and even days of
meticulous preparation. His dedication to his career is total, even
obsessive. Experience has not dimmed the intensity of his mind, nor the
10   intensity of his emotions, nor the volubility of his conversation. Partly
consciously, but mainly because it is part of his nature, he remains firmly
in the public eye, even in his hours of downfall and disgrace. . . .

By the end of 1933 Churchill was widely regarded as a failed politician,
in whom no real trust could be reasonably placed; by June 1935 these
15   opinions had been fortified further. His habit of exaggerating problems,
and in clothing relatively minor questions in brightly coloured language,
had the effect that when a really major issue did arise there was no easy
way of differentiating it. . . . His sense of the dramatic had ceased to
excite the emotions as it had once done – and was to do again in 1940. His
20   few political friends were neither collectively nor individually impressive
nor influential. . . .

Churchill's campaign for rearmament lacked the essential qualities of a
crusade. It was limited; it was personal; it was far from national; and it was
closely linked to the political fortunes of its leader. Great speeches in
25   Parliament and stirring public appeals do not constitute a crusade. This

was very much a politician's campaign, conducted in the main in the . . . Commons . . . before a highly sceptical . . . audience. Churchill did not at this time stand above party politics. He did not enjoy the privilege of being regarded as a national figure in the same sense as a
30 Pitt, a Burke, or a Gladstone. Perhaps the real cause of his failure was that he was regarded at large as just another politician, and by the . . . Commons as just another failed and disappointed politician.

These comments do not controvert Churchill's record on Defence matters in the years 1932–6. The inconstancies and errors of timing and
35 judgement do not seriously affect the central fact that he sensed danger long before most of his contemporaries discerned it. His principal theme was unanswerably right. But the failure of his campaign was not entirely the result of the folly of others. A dispassionate assessment of why his reputation remained so low at the end of 1936, after a period in which his
40 warnings had been proved to be abundantly justified, must return to the quotation. . . 'Every man is the maker of his own fate.'

R. R. James, *Churchill: A Study in Failure, 1900–1939,* Weidenfeld & Nicolson, 1970 [Penguin edn 1973], pp. 121–2, 358–9

Questions

a What posts had Churchill held 'over ten years of office' (line 2)?
b What were the 'hours of downfall and disgrace' (line 12) and how had they come about?
c In what way did Churchill's sense of the dramatic excite emotions in 1940 (lines 18–19)?
d Why was Churchill's clarion call on rearmament and the dangers from abroad largely ignored during the 1930s?
* e Who were Churchill's main supporters in the 1930s and what did he expect of them?
* f To what extent was mistrust of Churchill between the wars due to events before 1918, like Tonypandy (1910) and Gallipoli (1915)?
   g Examine the reasons given by R. R. James for his view that Churchill was a 'failed politician' (line 13) in the 1930s.

6 Churchill the Historian

Britain entered the twentieth century in the grip of war. She placed nearly half a million men in the field, the biggest force she had hitherto sent overseas throughout her history. The conflict . . . soon called for a large-scale national effort. Its course was followed . . . with intense
5 interest and lively emotion. Scarcely a generation had gone by since the Franchise Acts had granted a say in the affairs of State to every adult male. The power to follow events and to pass judgment upon them had recently come within the reach of all through free education. Popular journals had started to circulate among the masses, swiftly bringing
10 news . . . into millions of homes. Yet the result of this rapid diffusion of

knowledge and responsibility was not, as some had prophesied, social unrest and revolutionary agitation. On the contrary, the years of the Boer War saw a surge of patriotism among the vast majority of the British people, and a widespread enthusiasm for the cause of Empire. . . .

15 The general feeling in the country was staunchly Imperialist. There was pride in the broad crimson stretches on the map of the globe which marked the span of the British Empire, and confidence in the Royal Navy's command of the Seven Seas. Europe was envious. . . .

Nearly a hundred years of peace and progress had carried Britain to the
20 leadership of the world. She had striven repeatedly for the maintenance of peace, at any rate for herself, and progress and prosperity had been continuous in all classes. The franchise had been extended almost to the actuarial limit, and yet quiet and order reigned. Conservative forces had shown that they could ride the storm, and . . . that there was no great
25 storm between the domestic parties. . . . No one felt himself left out of the Constitution. An excess of self-assertion would be injurious. Certainly the dawn of the twentieth century seemed bright and calm for those who lived within the unequalled bounds of the British Empire, or sought shelter within its folds. There was endless work to be done. It did
30 not matter which party ruled: they found fault with one another, as they had a perfect right to do. None of the ancient inhibitions obstructed the adventurous. If mistakes were made they had been made before, and Britons could repair them without serious consequence. Active and vigorous politics should be sustained. To go forward gradually but
35 boldly seemed to be fully justified.

W. S. Churchill, *A History of the English-Speaking Peoples*, IV, *The Great Democracies*, Cassell, 1958 [but written before the Second World War], pp. 292–3, 303

Questions

a   Was it true to say that 'the Franchise Acts had granted a say . . . to every adult male' (lines 5–6)?

b   In building his image of *fin de siècle* Britain, what did Churchill omit in his comments on social unrest?

c   'For Churchill, the past confirmed the peculiar genius of the English race, and proved its right to be rich, Imperial, and the guardian of human freedoms.' (J. H. Plumb) What examples of that comment are visible here?

* d   Which policies had Churchill advocated while he was a Liberal Minister that illustrate his theme 'to go forward gradually but boldly' (lines 34–5) [cf. another title in this series *Nineteenth Century Britain*, chapter X]?

* e   Using Plumb's chapter in *Churchill: Four Faces and the Man*, and considering Sir Lewis Namier's comment to Churchill that 'Too much history is written by don-bred dons', discuss the merits of Churchill as an historian.

7 Their Finest Hour

What General Weygand called the Battle of France is over. I expect that the Battle of Britain is about to begin. Upon this battle depends the survival of Christian civilisation. Upon it depends our own British life, and the long continuity of our institutions and our Empire. The whole
5 fury and might of the enemy must very soon be turned on us. Hitler knows that he will have to break us in this island or lose the war. If we can stand up to him, all Europe may be free and the life of the world may move forward into broad, sunlit uplands. But if we fail, then the whole world, including the United States, including all that we have known and
10 cared for, will sink into the abyss of a new Dark Age made more sinister, and perhaps more protracted, by the lights of perverted science. Let us therefore brace ourselves to our duties, and so bear ourselves that, if the British Empire and its Commonwealth last for a thousand years, men will still say, 'This was their finest hour.'

15 The gratitude of every home in our Island, in our Empire, and indeed throughout the world, except in the abodes of the guilty, goes out to the British airmen who, undaunted by odds, unwearied in their constant challenge and mortal danger, are turning the tide of the world war by their prowess and by their devotion. Never in the field of human conflict
20 was so much owed by so many to so few. All hearts go out to the fighter pilots, whose brilliant actions we see with our own eyes day after day; but we must never forget that all the time, night after night, month after month, our bomber squadrons travel far into Germany, find their targets in the darkness by the highest navigational skill, aim their attacks, often
25 under the heaviest fire, often with serious loss, with deliberate careful discrimination, and inflict shattering blows upon the whole of the technical and war-making structure of the Nazi power. On no part of the Royal Air Force does the weight of the war fall more heavily than on the daylight bombers who will play an invaluable part in the case of invasion
30 and whose unflinching zeal it has been necessary in the meanwhile on numerous occasions to restrain. . . .

W. S. Churchill, *Into Battle*, Cassell, 1941, pp. 234, 259

Questions

a   From internal evidence, give an approximate date to these two speeches.
b   What aspects of these speeches made them particularly memorable? Why was this?
* c   Bearing in mind two of the events of 1940, what is the role of myth and legend in human affairs and in the study of history?
* d   Examine the record of Churchill as a war leader and strategist in the years 1940–45.

Further Work

a Consider the point that Chamberlain was a success until 1937, while Churchill was a failure until 1939.

b 'It was Churchill's greatest deficiency in the 1930s that he was unchanged; it was to be his greatest strength in the ordeal that began on 3 September 1939.' (R. R. James) Discuss this statement.

c 'All his life had been an unconscious preparation for this hour, and his qualities as a statesman must be judged principally from the way in which he discharged his trust during the Second World War.' (A. J. P. Taylor) What great qualities did Churchill reveal during the Second World War?

d 'A fallible, erratic, human being of immense ability but uneven judgement.' (R. R. James) Is this a useful starting-point on Churchill?

VI The Mythology of the Thirties — The Devil's Decade?

Introduction

Impression plays an important part in the historical process. This is certainly true of the inter-war period, especially the nineteen-thirties. Today of all periods of recent history the events of the thirties are most familiar to us. We have a clear, if oversimplified, impression of the decade, an impression reinforced by parental memory. Oral evidence tends to provide a very unreliable impression of that period, especially if the people interviewed actually lived through it as adults. The thirties is still shrouded in a deeply-felt mythology — the spectre of unemployment and the means test, the belief in the betrayal of the Labour Party by Ramsay MacDonald in 1931 and an unease that appeasement — still a politically dirty word — was so readily assented to. It is necessary for the historian to get behind this façade to see precisely what the problems of this period were and to see whether the popular impression is correct or not. That is the aim of this chapter.

George Orwell provides the historian with an invaluable, if somewhat emotive, picture of conditions in the depressed areas. He lays stress upon the real character of poverty based upon his own experiences and fieldwork. He highlights both the concerns of the working class and the apprehensions of the middle class as to the possible effects of depression. The spectre of Bolshevism was yet another facet to the mythology of the thirties. J. B. Priestley provides a useful corrective to a view which, as Orwell himself admitted later, emphasised the worst rather than the improving features of British society. Priestley shows that the 'two nations' view of the thirties was grossly oversimplified. There was certainly depression and appalling human suffering but it was localised rather than general.

This view is taken up by the other exorcists included in this chapter. L. J. Williams provides an economic historian's view of the inter-war period which emphasises the importance of growth within the economy. A. J. P. Taylor rightly sees the thirties as a period of paradox with politicians attempting to strengthen the weakened and declining remnants of industrial greatness, while the people were buying the 'new' industrial products — a good example of lack of real political communication. John Stevenson and Chris Cook show the difference between the myth and the reality of the depression and begin the process of de-mythologising the period. This process will probably be a long one as impressions always die hard.

This chapter stresses the importance of questioning received truths and of not accepting generalisations at face value. The historian should always go back to the evidence on which generalisations are based and re-examine it to see how accurate an impression it actually provides. The devil can take many forms!

Further Reading (For a fuller list on this topic, see pp. 82—3.)

B. W. E. Alford, *Depression and Recovery? British Economic Growth 1918—1939* (Macmillan, 1972), a good bibliographical study.

N. Branson & M. Heinemann, *Britain in the Nineteen Thirties* (Weidenfeld & Nicolson, 1971), a good analytical social history.

B. B. Gilbert, *British Social Policy 1914—1939* (Batsford, 1970), probably the definitive study.

C. L. Mowat, *Britain between the Wars 1918—1940* (Methuen, 1955), a good general survey of developments, though it has been superseded in some areas.

R. Skidelsky, *Politicians and the Slump* (Macmillan, 1967), a detailed study of attempts made to resolve the economic problems between 1929 and 1931.

J. Stevenson, *Social Conditions in Britain Between the Wars* (Penguin, 1977), a good attempt at getting behind the mythology of the twenties and thirties.

1 The Depression – a Pessimistic View

. . . The most cruel and evil effect of the Means Test is the way in which it breaks up families. Old people, sometimes bedridden, are driven out of their homes by it. An old age pensioner, for instance, if a widower, would normally live with one or other of his children; his weekly ten shillings goes towards the household expenses, and probably he is not badly cared for. Under the Means Test, however, he counts as a 'lodger' and if he stays at home his children's dole will be docked. . . .

Nevertheless, in spite of the frightful extent of unemployment, it is a fact that poverty – extreme poverty – is less in evidence in the industrial North than it is in London. Everything is poorer and shabbier, there are fewer motor-cars and fewer well-dressed people; but also there are fewer people who are obviously destitute. Even in a town the size of Liverpool or Manchester you are struck by the fewness of the beggars. London is a sort of whirlpool which draws derelict people towards it, and it is so vast that life there is solitary and anonymous. . . . But in the industrial towns the old communal way of life has not yet broken up, tradition is still strong and almost everyone has a family – potentially. . . . Moreover, there is just this to be said for the unemployment regulations, that they do not discourage people from marrying. A man and wife on twenty-three

shillings a week are not far from the starvation line, but they can make a
home of sorts; they are vastly better off than a single man on fifteen
shillings. The life for a single unemployed man is dreadful. He lives
sometimes in a common lodging-house, more often in a 'furnished' room
for which he usually pays six shillings a week, finding for himself as best
he can on the other nine (say six shillings a week for food and three for
clothes, tobacco, and amusements). Of course he cannot feed or look after
himself properly, and a man who pays six shillings a week for his room is
not encouraged to be indoors more than is necessary. So he spends his
days loafing in the public library or any other place where he can keep
warm. That − keeping warm − is almost the sole preoccupation of a
single unemployed man in winter. In Wigan a favourite refuge was the
pictures, which are fantastically cheap there. You can always get a seat for
fourpence, and at the matinée at some houses you can even get a seat for
twopence. Even people on the verge of starvation will readily pay
twopence to get out of the ghastly cold of a winter afternoon. In Sheffield
I was taken to a public hall to listen to a lecture by a clergyman I
found it physically impossible to sit it out, indeed my feet carried me out,
seemingly of their own accord, before it was half-way through. Yet the
hall was thronged with unemployed men; they would have sat through
far worse drivel for the sake of a warm place to shelter. . . .

    You can't settle to anything, you can't command the spirit of hope in
which anything has got to be created, with that dull evil cloud of
unemployment hanging over you. . . . There is no work to look for, and
everybody knows it. You can't go on looking for work every day for
seven years. There are allotments, which occupy the time and help to
feed the family, but in a big town there are only allotments for a small
proportion of the people. Then there are the occupational centres which
were started a few years ago to help the unemployed. . . . They say that
the occupational centres are simply a device to keep the unemployed
quiet and give them the illusion that something is being done for them.
Undoubtedly that *is* the underlying motive. Keep a man busy mending
boots and he is less likely to read the *Daily Worker*. . . . By far the best
work for the unemployed is being done by the N.U.W.M. − National
Unemployed Workers' Movement. . . .

    To study unemployment and its effects you have got to go to the
industrial areas. In the South unemployment exists, but it is scattered and
queerly unobtrusive. There are plenty of rural districts where a man out
of work is almost unheard-of, and you don't anywhere see the spectacle
of whole blocks of cities living on the dole and the P.A.C. . . . When I
first saw unemployed men at close quarters, the thing that horrified and
amazed me was to find that many of them were ashamed of being
unemployed. . . . The middle classes were still talking about 'lazy idle
loafers on the dole' and saying that 'these men could all find work if they
wanted to', and naturally these opinions percolated to the working class
themselves. . . .

    Twenty million people are underfed but literally everyone in England
has access to a radio. What we have lost in food we have gained in

electricity. Whole sections of the working class who have been plundered of all they really need are being compensated, in part, by cheap luxuries
70   which mitigate the surface of life.

George Orwell, *The Road to Wigan Pier*, 1937, Penguin edn 1971, pp. 70–76, 80

Questions

a (i) In the context of the 1920s what do the following words mean: 'Means Test' (line 1); 'dole' (line 7); 'unemployment regulations' (line 18); 'the starvation line' (line 20); 'common lodging-house' (line 23); 'allotments' (line 45) and 'P.A.C.' (line 59)?
(ii) Why did Orwell conclude that London was 'so vast that life there is solitary and anonymous' (lines 14–15)?
(iii) What is the significance of lines 51–2?

b Who was George Orwell and how reliable do you think this extract is as a piece of historical evidence?

c What information does Orwell provide the historian with about the incidence of unemployment and attempts to alleviate it?

*   *d* How important do you think the cinema was during the 1930s? What types of films were produced at this time and what was their social function?

*   *e* What was the National Unemployed Workers' Movement and what did it aim to do? Did it achieve its aims?

f Orwell provides the historian with only one side of what the 1930s were like. His work is therefore biased. The cause of this bias was his journalistic training. Discuss.

2   'The Three Englands' – a More Hopeful View

. . . I had seen England. I had seen a lot of Englands. How many? At once, three disengaged themselves from the shifting mass. There was, first, Old England, the country of the cathedrals and minsters and manor houses and inns, of Parson and Squire; guidebook and quaint highways and
5   byways England. . . . But we all know this England, which at its best cannot be improved upon in this world. . . .

Then, I decided, there is the nineteenth-century England, the industrial England of coal, iron, steel, cotton, wool, railways; of thousands of rows of little houses all alike, sham Gothic churches, square-faced chapels,
10   Town Halls, Mechanics' Institutes, mills, foundries, warehouses, refined watering-places, Pier Pavilions, Family and Commercial Hotels, Literary and Philosophical Societies, back-to-back houses, detached villas with monkey-trees, Grill Rooms, railway stations, slag-heaps and 'tips', dock roads, Refreshment Rooms, doss-houses, Unionist or Liberal Clubs,
15   cindery waste ground, mill chimneys, fried-fish shops, public-houses.
. . . This England makes up the larger part of the Midlands and the North

and exists everywhere; but it is not being added to and has no new life poured into it. To the more fortunate people it was not a bad England at all, very solid and comfortable . . . The third England, I concluded, was
20 the new post-war England, belonging far more to the age itself than to this island. America, I supposed, was its real birthplace. This is the England of arterial and by-pass roads, of filling stations and factories that look like exhibiting buildings, of giant cinemas and dance-halls and cafés, bungalows with tiny garages, cocktail bars, Woolworths, motor-
25 coaches, wireless, hiking, factory girls looking like actresses, greyhound racing and dirt tracks, swimming pools and everything given away for cigarette coupons. . . . Care is necessary too, for you can easily approve or disapprove of it too hastily. It is, of course, essentially demo-cratic. . . . You need money in this England, but you do not need
30 much money. It is a large-scale, mass-production job, with cut prices. You could almost accept Woolworths as its symbol. . . . In this England, for the first time in history, Jack and Jill are nearly as good as their master and mistress. . . . Most of the work . . . is rapidly becoming standar-dised in this new England, and its leisure is being handed over to
35 standardisation too. It is a cleaner, tidier, healthier, saner world than that of nineteenth century industrialism. . . .

Here then were the three Englands I had seen, the Old, the Nineteenth-Century and the New; and as I looked back on my journey I saw how these three were variously and most fascinatingly mingled in every part
40 of the country I had visited. . . . .

J. B. Priestley, *English Journey*, Heinemann, 1934, pp. 397–412; Priestley subtitled his work – *Being a rambling but truthful account of what one man saw and heard and felt and thought during a journey through England during the autumn of the year 1933*

Questions

a (i) What do the following mean: 'of Parson and Squire' (line 4); 'Mechanics' Institutes' (line 10); 'doss-houses' (line 14)?
(ii) In what ways had Priestley 'seen a lot of Englands' (line 1)?
(iii) Why does Priestley say that the North 'is not being added to and has no new life poured into it' (lines 17–18)?
(iv) Why does he say of the 'New' England that 'You could almost accept Woolworths as its symbol' (line 31)?
(v) In what ways was much work in the 'New' England 'rapidly becoming standardised' (lines 33–4)?
b Who is J. B. Priestley and how reliable do you think this extract is as a piece of historical evidence?
c What literary techniques does Priestley use to make the reader aware of the differences between his three Englands? How successful do you think this technique is?
* d Priestley provides a clearer and less one-sided picture than Orwell of the diversity of England in the 1930s. Discuss.

* e Two of Priestley's Englands were home-grown while the third was an American import. How valid an assertion is this?

3 The Economic Position – the 1920s and 1930s Compared

In terms of general economic growth, the 1930's seem to have been similar to the 1920's, or at least to the period from 1924 to 1929. The rate of growth of total output (about 2.2 per cent), total employment (1.3 per cent) and output per employee (0.9 per cent) was very much the same
5 between 1924–29 and 1929–37. If the totals are broken down some differences emerge – output in manufactures and distribution grew faster in the 1930's, while construction and primary industries grew more slowly than in the 1920's. But the major point to notice is that the overall growth performance was broadly similar over most of the inter-war
10 years, and that growth performance compared favourably with the immediate pre-1913 experience, returning to something like the level achieved during the second half of the nineteenth century. . . .

However, despite these statistical and aggregative similarities between the 1920's and 1930's, there are still some cogent reasons for arguing that,
15 for most of the people involved, the economic experience of the 1930's was more favourable. In part this was simply because the upward direction of the economy was more perceptible. Contemporaries seemed more conscious of improvement than they had been in the previous decade, although no doubt some of the consciousness was illusory and
20 arose partly because the depth of the depression in 1932 had been so severe.

There seem also to have been greater steps made towards adjusting the industrial structure. This again was to some degree only psychological in that, as time went on, there was a greater degree of acceptance of the
25 necessity for some sector to decline. No doubt this consideration also helps to explain why industrial relations in the 1930's were comparatively placid, in sharp contrast to the massive and bitter strife of the 1920's. Similarly, although the size and nature of the unemployment problem changed comparatively little – and mainly for the worse – there was,
30 with the flood of writing, research and social heart-searching on the topic, a much greater awareness of the basically localised and structural nature of the unemployment problem.

Finally, there was no doubting the much improved performance of the British economy relative to that of most other industrial countries. In the
35 general international upsurge of the years between 1925 and 1929 Britain had lagged markedly; but the British recovery which set in from 1932 was much more confident and perceptible than the faltering revivals in France and the United States (and although the same would not be true of Germany or the Soviet Union, few in Britain were prepared to accept the
40 human costs which their expansions entailed). Most of these consider- ations had little effect on the real level of activity; but if the factors which

seem to make the economic climate of the 1930's preferable to that of the 1920's are largely psychological, so too is the welfare that material and economic progress is meant to improve.

L. J. Williams, *Britain and the World Economy 1919–1970*, Fontana 1971, pp. 83–4

Questions

a (i) What does the author mean by the following: 'general economic growth' (line 1); 'total output' (line 3); 'output per employee' (line 4); 'statistical and aggregative similarities' (line 13)?
(ii) What were the 'greater steps' being made 'towards adjusting the industrial structure' (lines 22–3)?
(iii) Explain the reference to 'the massive and bitter strife of the 1920's (line 27).
(iv) In what ways was there 'a much greater awareness . . . of the unemployment problem' (lines 31–2)?
(v) Why did the economic revivals of Germany and the Soviet Union involve such 'human costs' (lines 39–40)?

b The picture which the economic historian provides of the 1920s and 1930s is different from that of the social historian. Why?

c The key to understanding the problems of the 1930s lies in the fact that 'output in manufactures and distribution grew faster . . . primary industries grew more slowly than in the 1920's' (lines 6–8). Discuss.

d Was the economic revival of the 1930s illusory and psychological rather than actual?

* e Why was the British economy able to revive more rapidly in the 1930s than did the economies of France and the United States?

4 The Thirties – an Appraisal

September 1931 marked the watershed of English history between the wars. . . . The break can be defined in many ways. The end of the gold standard was the most obvious and the most immediate. Until 21 September 1931 men were hoping somehow to restore the self-operating
5 economy which had existed, or was supposed to have existed, before 1914. After that day, they had to face conscious direction at any rate so far as money was concerned. . . .

Reconstruction, Restoration, Recovery were the key words of the twenties. . . . Nineteen-fourteen was the standard by which everything
10 was judged. Planning was the key word of the thirties: planned economy, plan for peace, planned families, plan for holidays. The standard was Utopia. . . .

Politicians strove to revive the depressed areas; the inhabitants left them. Public policy concentrated on the staple industries and on exports.
15 Capital and labour developed new industries which provided goods for

the home market. The government tried to promote new investment
abroad. The individual spent his money on domestic comforts – indeed,
with the growth of hire-purchase, spent other people's money also.
Similarly, the people lost interest in the empire and showed it in a
20 practical way. Whereas in the nineteen-twenties something like 100,000
people went overseas each year, in the thirties an average of over 20,000
returned home. In the words of Geoffrey Crowther, the English people
were 'more planned against than planning'. . . .
    The same sort of problem arises at every turn. Public affairs were harsh
25 and intense; private lives increasingly agreeable. The nineteen-thirties
have been called the black years, the devil's decade. Its popular image can
be expressed in two phrases: mass unemployment and 'appeasement'. No
set of political leaders have been judged so contemptuously since the days
of Lord North. Yet at the same time, most English people were enjoying
30 a richer life than any previously known in the history of the world: longer
holidays, shorter hours, higher real wages. They had the motor car,
cinemas, radio sets, electrical appliances. The two sides of life did not join
up. The public men themselves had the air of appearing in a charade. The
members of the National Government may be seen in a newsreel,
35 assembling for discussion: stern features, teeth clenched, as they face the
crisis. They would hesitate at nothing to save the country, to save the
pound. The result of their courage was that the children of the
unemployed had less margarine on their bread. After this resolute
decision, ministers dispersed to their warm, comfortable homes and ate
40 substantial meals. Such was 'equality of sacrifice'.

A. J. P. Taylor, *English History 1914–1945*, OUP [Penguin edn
1970], pp. 374–5, 377, 396

Questions

a (i) What does Taylor mean by the following: 'gold standard' (lines
2–3); 'the self-operating economy' (lines 4–5); 'Reconstruction'
(line 8); 'appeasement' (line 27); 'real wages' (line 31)?
(ii) What were the staple industries and the new industries and how
did they differ (lines 14–15)?
(iii) What is meant by 'the National Government' and why was it
formed (line 34)?
(iv) In what sense was 'the standard' of the thirties 'Utopia' (lines
11–12)?

b Who is A. J. P. Taylor and what does this passage tell you about his
views as a historian?

c Did September 1931 mark 'the watershed of English history between
the wars' (lines 1–2)?

d What does Taylor see as the fundamental differences between the
twenties and the thirties? Do you agree?

e How accurate is the epithet 'the devil's decade' (line 26) as a
description of the thirties?

* f Why have the political leaders of the thirties been judged 'so
contemptuously' (line 28)?

5 The Thirties – Myth and Reality

Of all periods in recent British history, the thirties have had the worst press. Although the decade can now only be remembered by the middle-aged and the elderly, it retains the all-pervasive image of the 'wasted years' and the 'low dishonest decade'. Even for those who did not live through them, the 1930's are haunted by the spectres of mass unemployment, hunger marches, appeasement, and the rise of fascism at home and abroad.

Mass unemployment, more than anything else, gave the inter-war period its image as the 'long weekend'. For almost twenty years there were never fewer than a million people out of work. . . . In the 1920's heavy unemployment reflected the special problems of the 'ailing giants', the staple export industries. . . . Their dislocation as a result of foreign competition and the contraction of world trade led to depression and unemployment in the old industrial areas. By 1929, the depression was a major political issue. The General Election of that year was fought primarily on domestic policy and resulted in a Labour Government under Ramsay MacDonald, pledged to conquer unemployment and restore the nation's prosperity.

It was not to be. Almost as soon as it came into office in June 1929, the new government began to be affected by the international crisis which has been called the 'Great Slump'. The promise of recovery in the depressed industries, and of a reduction of unemployment, was swept aside by the consequences of the Wall Street crash of October 1929. The immediate consequence was a rise in world-wide unemployment. By the middle of 1930 there were estimated to be over 11 million unemployed in 33 countries, double the figure before the onset of the slump. Britain was no exception. The country's exports were almost halved in value between 1929 and 1931. The industries which had been depressed in the 1920's now had to face an economic blizzard of unprecedented severity, but the slump also affected almost every branch of business activity. Instead of falling, the unemployment figures continued to rise; by July 1930 there were over 2 million people out of work.

In May 1931, the failure of the Vienna Bank, the Credit Anstalt, sparked off a crisis of confidence in Germany and a run on the Reichsbank. When the ripples of the European banking crisis spread to Britain, the Labour Government was already in dire straits. . . . Unable to agree upon a programme of economy measures, the Labour Government resigned. Ramsay MacDonald and a small group of Labour M.P.s joined the Conservatives to form a 'National' Government on 24 August.

The new government's tenure was confirmed two months later in a General Election which gave it a crushing majority of 497 seats and reduced the Labour Party to 52 seats in the House of Commons. It did not, however, end the economic crisis. Within a month of its formation the National Government was forced to abandon the Gold Standard. But

the worst effects of the international slump were still to be felt. Unemployment continued to rise through the winter of 1931−2, reaching a peak in the third quarter of 1932 when there were almost 3
50 million people out of work in Great Britain. The government's response was to implement economy measures, including cuts in unemployment benefit and the introduction of the means test. Financial orthodoxy and economic conservatism became the dominant features of its strategy to cope with the slump. . . .

55 In a sense the intervention of the Second World War served to perpetuate the more depressing image of the thirties, partly at least because the politics of the immediate post-war era were fought on the record of the pre-war years. As late as 1951 the Labour Party campaigned with the election slogan of 'Ask your Dad!' an illustration of the way in
60 which the emotive image of the 'hungry thirties' had become part of the repertoire of political cliché. The popular view of the 1930's as a period of unrelieved failure was undoubtedly hardened and reinforced in the years after the war; a view which became sharpened against the background of full employment and affluence of the 1950's and 1960's. Even today the
65 ghost of the thirties stalks political platforms and the media as a symbol of economic disaster, social deprivation and political discontent. . . . A concentration upon unemployment and social distress does not represent an accurate portrayal of the decade. . . . It would, of course, be fatuous to suggest that the 1930's were not for many thousands of people a time of
70 great hardship and personal suffering. But beside the picture of the unemployed must be put the other side of the case. . . . Alongside the picture of the dole queues and hunger marches must also be placed those of another Britain, of new industries, prosperous suburbs and a rising standard of living. . . . This was the paradox which lay at the heart of
75 Britain in the thirties . . . .

> John Stevenson and Chris Cook, *The Slump — society and politics during the Depression*, Cape, 1977, pp. 1−4.

Questions

a   (i) What were the 'special problems of the "ailing giants" ' (lines 10−11)?

(ii) Who was Ramsay MacDonald (line 17) and what role did he play in the politics of the 1920s and 1930s?

(iii) What was 'the Wall Street crash' (line 23) and what consequences did it have?

(iv) What were 'The country's exports' (line 27) in the late twenties?

(v) What were 'the economy measures' which the government introduced from 1931 (line 51)?

(vi) What did 'financial orthodoxy and economic conservatism' (lines 52−3) mean in the thirties?

(vii) What was the significance of the 1951 Labour election slogan (line 59)?

b   Why have the thirties had such a 'bad press' from historians?

* *c* The difference between the myth and the reality of the thirties leaves the historian with a paradox which has not yet been sufficiently explored. Discuss.
* *d* Present-day attitudes to depression are still highly influenced by the psychological impact of the thirties. Do you agree?
  e Do Stevenson and Cook provide a new beginning for historical analysis of the thirties?

Further Reading

The thirties is a decade well served with studies of its economic and social structure. On the inter-war economy see:

* D. H. Aldcroft *The Inter-war Economy: Britain 1919−1939* (London, 1969)

B. W. E. Alford *Depression and Recovery? British Economic Growth 1918−1939* (Macmillan, 1972), a good bibliographical study.

S. Glynn and J. Oxborrow *Interwar Britain: an Economic and Social History* (London, 1976), a recent study with good up-to-date interpretations.
On the society of the thirties:

N. Branson and M. Heinemann *Britain in the Nineteen Thirties* (Weidenfeld & Nicolson, 1971).

A. Marwick *Class: Image and Reality* (Collins, 1979), an interesting, eminently readable comparative study of class and its perception in Britain, France and USA, using a wide variety of sources; the first part deals with the thirties.

J. Stevenson *Social Conditions in Britain between the Wars* (Penguin, 1977), a good attempt at getting behind the mythology of the twenties and thirties.

On the social problems of this period (in addition to the books by R. C: Birch and D. Fraser cited in chapter VIII):

S. Constantine *Unemployment in Britain between the Wars* (Longman, 1980)

* B. B. Gilbert *British Social Policy 1914−1939* (Batsford, 1970), perhaps the definitive study.

R. Skidelsky *Politicians and the Slump* (Macmillan, 1967), a detailed study of attempts to resolve economic and social problems between 1929 and 1931.

E. Wilkinson *The Town that was Murdered* (Gollancz, 1939), a partisan account of Jarrow by its MP.

In addition to written sources the student is urged to look at visual evidence. Marwick's book cited above provides a useful analysis of films as a source of evidence. Nicholas Pronay has edited a series, *History through the Newsreel: the 1930s*, Macmillan 1976, and the film on *The Unemployed* will be found particularly useful.

On the politics of the thirties the most useful study is

J. Stevenson and C. Cook *The Slump: Society and Politics during the Depression*, London, 1977

although

P. Addison *The Road to 1945* (London, 1975) has much of value to say.

For the extremist movements of the 1930s see:

R. Benewick *The Fascist Movement in Britain* (London, 2nd edition, 1972)

H. Pelling *The British Communist Party* (London, 1976)

R. Skidelsky *Oswald Mosley* (Macmillan, 1975), the best study of this enigmatic figure though it has been criticised for being over-sympathetic to the subject.

VII   *Expediency And Morality: The Appeasement Debate*

Introduction

In the mid-1960s Martin Gilbert wrote:

'Munich' and appeasement' have both become words of disapproval and abuse. For nearly thirty years they have been linked together as the twin symbols of British folly. Together they have been defended as if they were inseparable. Yet 'Munich' was a policy, dictated by fear and weakness, which Neville Chamberlain devised as a means, not of postponing war but, as he personally believed, of making Anglo-German war unnecessary in the future. Appeasement was quite different; it was a policy of constant concessions based on common sense and strength.

By the mid-1970s the flood of evidence available after the Public Record Act of 1967 had led Gilbert to rethink his earlier views:

I had not realized the extent to which Neville Chamberlain's Cabinet were prepared to deceive Parliament. I had not realized the extent to which they chose to ignore the evidence of Hitler's intention put before them. . . . And finally, no one had then realized the extent to which, after Munich, far from using the so-called 'year gained' to re-arm, Chamberlain had adopted a quite different policy and a quite different attitude, that *now* the time had come for a real agreement with Hitler which would make massive rearmament unnecessary, and *dis*armament a possibility. And I document them both from the Cabinet and the Cabinet committee meetings . . . and also in Chamberlain's letters to his sister. . . .

The shadow of the First World War and the Versailles settlement hangs heavily over this chapter. Keynes' apparently damning indictments and the vigour of the French (as, for example, in the occupation of the Ruhr) helped to develop the policy of appeasement, often misunderstood, as Gilbert mentioned, with the policy of fear of 1937–9. Appeasement had a coherent intellectual foundation with a high moral tone, but the aggressive expansionist policies of Mussolini in Abyssinia and Hitler in Central Europe exposed the absence of force to substantiate its principles. By 1937 there was a bitter ideological debate on appeasement, reflected in G. M. Trevelyan's letter to *The Times*. The following year the policy soured, but not before substantial British and Dominion support for the 'resolution' of the Czechoslovak crisis at Munich. The bitterness of comments from France and Czechoslovakia also reflects the continental feeling that Britain's geography enabled her to see Europe from too detached and moralistic a viewpoint; in view of France's internal weaknesses, and the emergence of the Czechoslovak state in 1918 when Germany was weak, these arguments may have less weight in retrospect.

One very interesting area for the modern historian is the newsreels of the 1930s. The miles of footage offer many examples of the moulding of public opinion by the five main newsreel companies, and the example in this chapter is but a pale reflection in print of what is on celluloid. The power of the newsreels in the Munich crisis should be apparent, however, and the involvement of the 'common man' in seeing the events almost as they happened marks a new stage in the history of Britain in the twentieth century.

Further Reading

A. Adamthwaite (ed.), *The Making of the Second World War* (Allen and Unwin, 1977), a politico-diplomatic collection of documents with a readable analytical introduction, designed for A-level use.

W. S. Churchill, *The Gathering Storm* (Cassell, 1948), the Churchillian interpretation of the inter-war period with definite views on the author's role.

W. R. Rock, *British Appeasement in the 1930s* (Arnold, 1977), a balanced and reasonably short assessment of the personalities and policies of the appeasers and their critics, perhaps overemphasising the role of Chamberlain.

C. Thorne, *The Approach of War, 1938–1939* (Macmillan, 1967), a brief narrative of the climax of appeasement.

D. C. Watt, 'The Historiography of Appeasement' in A. Sked and C. Cook (eds), *Crisis and Controversy: Essays in Honour of A. J. P. Taylor* (Macmillan, 1976), a review of the appeasement debate, which relates the historians and their points of view to the context of the post-war world. Highly recommended for more detailed study of the topic.

The use of the following is also recommended. Both are obtainable on loan.

The Munich Crisis (a documentary film) British Universities Historical Studies in Film

If War Should Come (a short compilation of newsreel extracts) Macmillan Education/The Historical Association

1 The Carthaginian Peace

Moved by insane delusion and reckless self-regard, the German people overturned the foundations on which we all lived and built. But the spokesmen of the French and British peoples have run the risk of completing the ruin. . . . Paris was a nightmare. . . . A sense of impending catastrophe overhung the frivolous scene. . . . Seated indeed amid the theatrical trappings of the French Saloons of State, one could wonder if the extraordinary visages of Wilson and of Clemenceau, with their fixed hue and unchanging characterisation, were really faces at all and not the tragi-comic masks of some strange drama or puppet-show. . . .

10   In spite . . . of France's victorious issue from the present
struggle . . . her future position remained precarious in the eyes of one
[Clemenceau] who took the view that European civil war is to be
regarded as a normal, or at least a recurrent, state of affairs for the
future. . . . Hence the necessity of 'guarantees'; and each guarantee that
15   was taken, by increasing irritation and thus the probability of a
subsequent *Revanche* by Germany, made necessary yet further provisions
to crush. Thus . . . a demand for a Carthaginian peace is
inevitable. . . . By loss of territory and other measures [Germany's]
population was to be curtailed; but chiefly the economic system . . . the
20   vast fabric built upon iron, coal, and transport, must be destroyed. . . .
It is evident that Germany's pre-war capacity to pay an annual foreign
tribute has not been unaffected by the almost total loss of her colonies, her
overseas connections, her mercantile marine, and her foreign properties,
by the cession of ten per cent of her territory and population, of one-third
25   of her coal and of three-quarters of her iron ore, by two million casualties
amongst men in the prime of life, by the starvation of her people for four
years, by the burden of a vast war debt, by the depreciation of her
currency to less than one-seventh its former value, by the disruption of
her allies and their territories, by Revolution at home and Bolshevism on
30   her borders, and by all the unmeasured ruin in strength and hope of four
years of all-swallowing war and final defeat.
All this, one would have supposed, is evident. Yet most estimates of a
great indemnity from Germany depend on the assumption that she is in a
position to conduct in the future a vastly greater trade than ever she has
35   had in the past. . . .
We cannot expect to legislate for a generation or more. . . . We
cannot as reasonable men do better than base our policy on the evidence
we have and adapt it to the five or ten years over which we may suppose
ourselves to have some measure of prevision. . . . The fact that we have
40   no adequate knowledge of Germany's capacity to pay over a long period
of years is no justification . . . for the statement that she can pay ten
thousand million pounds.
If we aim deliberately at the impoverishment of Central Europe,
vengeance, I dare predict, will not limp. Nothing can then delay for very
45   long that final civil war between the forces of Reaction and the despairing
convulsions of Revolution, before which the horrors of the late German
war will fade into nothing, and which will destroy, whoever is victor, the
civilisation and the progress of our generation. . . .
J. M. Keynes, *The Economic Consequences of the Peace*, Macmillan
1919 [1924 edn], pp. 1, 3–4, 31–2, 173, 190, 251

Questions

a   Explain '*Revanche*' (line 16) and 'Carthaginian peace' (line 17).
b   Why did Keynes think that it was both economically unsound and
politically unwise to ask Germany for high reparations? Examine the
validity of his comments.

c What did Keynes predict as the probable outcome of trying to legislate for more than a generation? Was his view held by many others in 1919?

* *d* 'Keynes destroyed British faith in Versailles. He opened the floodgates of criticism. For the next twenty years the Treaty was assailed by means of his arguments.' (M. Gilbert) Examine the impact of this book on British foreign policy in the 1920s.

* *e* Using Chapters I and II from *Twentieth Century Europe* in this series, comment on Keynes' criticisms of the events in Paris and the aims of the 'Big Four'. Did he underestimate the difficulties of peacemaking in 1919?

* *f* Attempt a reply to Keynes from the standpoint of (a) a Frenchman in 1919; (b) a Weimar Republic politician and (c) a present-day historian or economist.

2 Newsreels

BBC series script: Unless we understand the significance of [the] cinematographic image of Neville Chamberlain it is impossible to understand either his considerable popularity or the trust he inspired in the hearts of ordinary people, and without this the Munich Crisis of
5 September 1938 would hardly have taken the turn it did.

Gaumont-British, September 1938: The hour of need has found the man, Mr Neville Chamberlain, the Prime Minister. Since he took office Mr Chamberlain has never wavered in his determination to establish peace in Europe. At the hour when the dark clouds of war hung most menacingly
10 above the world of men, the Prime Minister took a wise and bold decision. Well may we call him Chamberlain the Peacemaker. Lord Halifax, the Foreign Secretary, was at Heston to see the Premier off on this epic-making flight to Germany, the first flight he has ever made. We know that no man could do more than he, but since we also know that it
15 lies not in the power of mortals to command success, we say with all our hearts, 'May God go with him!' Three cheers for Chamberlain!...

BBC series script: Everything depended at this stage on whether Chamberlain could get and keep the public's support for what was in fact an unprecedented personal deal with a foreign dictator. The newsreels
20 were using the image *they* had built up to justify their giving him unqualified support before the negotiations had even *begun*, let alone succeeded. Years of hard work [by Chamberlain in forging close links with the newsreels and of mastering the technique of creating a cinematic image as the champion of the ordinary man's viewpoint] finally paid off.
25 The Munich Crisis was also the first major crisis covered by the newsreels. British newsreel companies co-operated with the German Ministry of Propaganda to provide massive coverage of Chamberlain's three visits to Hitler.... The massive coverage of the crisis provided the cinema audience with a diet of mounting excitement. The now famous newsreel
30 of Chamberlain's return from Munich is both the climax of the media campaign and historical evidence of its result....

Gaumont-British, October 1938:

Picture	Commentary	Sound

PEACE INSTEAD OF WAR

35   Twenty-four years ago there was a war to end war. How soon we   'O God, our help in

Trenches   learned that that was just a dream.   ages past'

Cenotaph   Millions of young men gave their

On-screen   lives, then the world recovered, but

40   *caption:*   scarely had the wheels of industry

PEACE   begun to turn again when the house

On-screen   of cards came crashing down once

caption: more.

BUT WAS IT

45   PEACE?

On-screen
captions,
(Superimposed
over film from   War sound
50   Manchuria,   effects and
Abyssinia, Spain   mood music
and China):

1932
MANCHUKUO
55   1935
ABYSSINIA
1936
SPAIN
1937
60   CHINA

On-screen
caption:
ONE MAN SAVED   So our Prime Minister has come
US FROM THE   back from his third and greatest
65   GREATEST WAR   journey and he said that 'the settle-
OF ALL   ment of the Czechoslovakian prob-
Caption fades   lem which has now been achieved is,
into film of   in my view, only the prelude to a
Chamberlain at   larger settlement in which all
70   Heston Airport   Europe may find peace.   Cheers
                      'This morning I had another talk
with the German Chancellor, Herr
Hitler, and here is the paper which
bears his name upon it as well as
75   mine. Some of you, perhaps, have

already heard what it contains, but I
would just like to read it to you: Cheers

"We, the German Führer and
Chancellor, and the British Prime
80   Minister, have had a further meeting
today and are agreed in recognising
that the question of Anglo-German
relations is of the first importance for
the two countries and for Europe.
85   We regard the agreement signed last
night and the Anglo-German Naval
agreement as symbolic of the desire
of our two peoples never to go to
war with one another again." '   Cheers

90   There was no sign of British
reserve as the crowds fought to get
near the Premier's car. As we travelled back with Mr Chamberlain from
Heston we drove through serried
95   masses of happy people, happy in the
knowledge that there was no war
with Germany.   Cheers

The Premier drove straight to
Buckingham Palace; here he was
100   received by the King while London
waited. And history was made again
when their Majesties came out on to
that famous balcony with the Prime   'Land of
Minister.   Hope and
105   Posterity will thank God, as we   Glory'
do now, that in the time of desperate
need our safety was guarded by such
a man: Neville Chamberlain.

Illusions of Reality: 2, Men of the Hour, BBC Continuing
Education TV written by Nicholas Pronay and produced by
Howard Smith

Questions

a   The commentary mentions Chamberlain returning from 'his third
and greatest journey' (lines 64–5). What had happened on the other
two, and what settlement was reached at Munich?

b   How valid is the juxtaposition of the events on lines 48–60?

c   How did the newsreel of the return of Chamberlain from Munich
support his peacemaking efforts? Include examples of pictures,
commentary and sound.

*   d   A piece of film is not some unadulterated reflection of historical truth captured
by the camera which does not require the interposition of the historian. (J. A.
S. Grenville)

The Newsreels laid stress on the points of similarity, identity of outlook and interest between the world of the government and that of the working-class regulars. Above all, they stressed the points of consensus rather than the points of conflict. (Nicholas Pronay)

What questions should the historian ask about the newsreels and their audiences?

* e Investigate, using the BBC *Illusions of Reality* programme, the 'cinematographic image of Neville Chamberlain' (line 2) built up by the newsreel companies when he was Chancellor of the Exchequer and Prime Minister.

* f Has this section on propaganda and newsreels any lessons or guidance for the 1980s?

* g What was the role of government in determining the content of newsreels?

3 Perfidious Albion?

LE GOUVERNEMENT FRANÇAIS RENFORCE SES MESURES DE PRECAUTION
Certaines catégories de réservistes ont été rappelées d'urgence

Il est bien inutile de vouloir dissimuler la verité. Elle est éclatante. La
5 France a subi, voici quelque jours, une humiliation sans précédent. La presse allemagne a parlé de 'Sedan diplomatique' . . . . Nous nous sommes inclinés devant la menace. Nous avons cédé au chantage. La revendication allemande est devenue le plan franco-britannique et . . . les deux grandes démocraties sont allées jusqu'à faire pression sur la
10 Tchécoslovaquie pour qu'elle se sacrifie. Si puissants que soient les motifs qui ont dicté leur décision aux gouvernants responsables de London et de Paris, le peuple français n'a pas caché sa douleur d'une pareille capitulation.

Cette politique de faiblesse, loin d'aplanir les difficultés, n'a fait
15 qu'exalter l'orgueil allemand et accroître les exigences de Hitler jusqu'à les rendre insupportables. . . .

Comment en sommes-nous arrivés là? Il serait injuste de rejeter toute la responsabilité de cette situation sur le gouvernement français. Celui-ci, en effet, a dû faire face a dès difficultés multiples et d' origine déjà ancienne.
20 L'opinion publique s'est montrée très divisée. Un conflit d'idéologies a empêché l'unanimité française de se réaliser derrière le gouvernement. La hantise du communisme a conduit certains éléments nationaux à méconnaître le danger allemand. Des polémiques infiniment regrettables se sont instituées sue les droits respectifs des Tchèques et des Sudètes.
25 Tandis que le gouvernement disait: 'Nous ne permettrons pas qu'on attaque la Tchécoslovaquie', il y avait chez nous des gens pour affirmer que: 'Nous ne nous battrions pas pour les Tchèques.' Et cette affirmation était d'autant plus désastreuse qu'on la retrouvait sous la plume d'hommes qui avaient occupé les plus hauts postes de l'Etat. 'C'est un grand malheur

30   pour un pays . . . d'être divisé sur sa politique étrangère.' Hélas! nous
    l'avons bien vu.
        Par ailleurs, les désordres sociaux qui se sont perpétués pendant toute la
    période de tension diplomatique ne pouvaient qu'encourager l'adversaire
    dans son audace. . . .
35   Signalons enfin l'attitude singulière des communistes au cours de cette
    crise. Chaque jour, dans *L'Humanité*, on pouvait lire des appels enflammés
    à la résistance, de pathétiques développements sur la grandeur de la
    patrie. . . . Mais chaque jour aussi . . . on pouvait lire des encourage-
    ments à la grève, des attaques partisanes contre le gouvernement, l'énoncé
40   de revendications nouvelles susceptibles de créer de nouveaux conflits
    sociaux . . . .
        De son côté, l'Angleterre . . . a manifesté de bien troublantes
    hésitations.
        L'Angleterre a compris tardivement la caractère européen du prob-
45   lème posé. Elle a cru qu'il y avait seulement un problème sudète à
    résoudre, une simple question de minorités. Elle a mis quelque temps à se
    rendre compte que le sort de l'Europe et son propre sort étaient
    directement en jeu. Les tendances insulaires sont chez elles si profondes
    qu'elle ne réalise que lentement la solidarité de fait qui l'unit à l'Europe
50   continentale. Elle s'est aperçue bien tard que la frontière de l'Empire
    n'était pas sur les côtes de la Manche, mais sur le Rhin. Elle aurait dû aussi
    comprendre plus tôt qu'en l'espèce, sa frontière comme la nôtre, était sur
    les monts de Bohème.
        Et puis, l'action diplomatique moderne est trop dépendante de la force
55   militaire de l'Etat pour que l'Angleterre puisse, sans posséder d'armée,
    remplir pleinement son rôle dans la politique continentale. Les démarches
    de son ambassadeur à Berlin auraient eu singulièrement plus de poids si le
    peuple anglais avait été soumis à la conscription . . . .
        Paul Simon in the regional newspaper *L'Ouest Eclair*, 15, 2904, 26
        September 1938, p. 1

Questions

a   What was meant by a 'Sedan diplomatique' (line 6)?

b   According to this provincial newspaper, what had the policy of
    weakness over Czechoslovakia led to?

c   What role had the French communists and the fear of communism in
    France played in the crisis?

* *d*   Comment on the French reaction to British policies in 1938 (lines
    42−58). How does this relate to French security between the wars
    (cf. *Twentieth Century Europe*, chapter V)?

* *e*   Examine the problems of French internal and external policies in the
    1930s. Were there any echoes in Britain of 'Nous ne nous battrions
    pas pour les Tchèques' (line 27)?

* *f*   What does this document say, either as 'witting' or 'unwitting'
    testimony, on national viewpoints and on the role of Britain in
    Europe?

4 Crisis in Prague

The Times had that very morning [7 September 1938] published its
explosive article . . . . It foresaw that the Sudeten Germans might
deliberately demand more than Prague could possibly yield, thus proving
that they were not 'at ease' in Czechoslovakia. 'In that case', the article
5   stated . . . 'it might be worth while for the Czechoslovak Government to
consider whether they should exclude altogether the project . . . of
making Czechoslovakia a more homogeneous state by the secession of that
fringe of alien populations who are contiguous to that nation with which
they are united by race.' In other words, Prague should let the Sudeten
10   lands go outright to Germany . . . .

Everywhere I went in Prague during the next few days I was pounced
upon by officials, diplomats and journalists. I could shake very few of
them out of their treasured opinion that *The Times* was the direct voice of
the British Government. . . . Given the standing and great influence of
15   *The Times* in those years . . . I knew the damage would be at least as great
as if the article had been inspired directly by the Government. . . . The
article was a signal that Chamberlain had allies. . . .

Geoffrey Dawson was of course in sympathy with Chamberlain and
Halifax. . . . His deputy editor . . . was carried forward by a burning
20   mission to save the world from another war . . . . Like Halifax, he told
me more than once that Germany was ordained to exert influence over
central and eastern Europe. . . .

It was . . . on September 21, that the people of Prague decided . . . to
take a direct hand in events. Very quickly crowds began to gather
25   in . . . Wenceslas Square. . . . At first they stood about in threes and
fours, reading the papers and arguing. Some larger groups were mainly
young men and girls, shabbily dressed. Soon men and women came in
hundreds, then thousands, filling the square. They began by seeming
wholly bewildered. Many were weeping. 'What fools we were to spend
30   such money on frontier defences', I heard one man say, but few followed
that line. 'We don't need any more guarantees,' said another, 'we want
aeroplanes.' A well dressed woman stopped, guessing that I was British.
'Each night,' she said in a cultured voice, 'I pray that Heaven may punish
France for her treachery and Britain for her blindness.' . . .
35   Still without anyone giving orders the crowds began moving out of
the bottom end of the square, shouting and singing the national anthem.
Police said there were two hundred thousand on the streets . . .

In front of the [Hradcany] Palace the people called again for General
Syrovy, the highly popular Inspector General of the Forces, to take over
40   and for all concessions to be stopped. Then the shouting changed. It took
on a deeper meaning that caught one's breath. 'Tell us the *truth*. We want
the *truth*.' It was a sovereign demand . . . .

A few days later the people showed their will more
formidably . . . . [It was announced at 10.20 p.m. on 25 September
45   that] all classes of men under 40 [were] to report immediately to their
military depots. . . . In 10 minutes the whole of the broad boulevard,

which had been as bright as Piccadilly with moving cars, became dark as a
mass of men, walking shoulder to shoulder the whole width of the
thoroughfare, pressed on to the station. In place of the noise of trains and
cars all one heard was the heavy swish and slur of hundreds of shoes. Some
women walked with the men, the older ones tearful, the younger ones
proudly holding on to the arms of their fathers and husbands. 'Well, it
had to come.' 'We won't let those German brutes through.' . . .

The third demonstration . . . came a few days later. It is something
any westerner would wish he had not seen. Munich had happened.
Threatened with immediate war with Germany, and told by Britain and
France that Czechoslovakia would be left to founder alone unless she
submitted, Dr Benesh and his Ministers surrendered. Long sleeplessness
and hours of browbeating from friends and allies had brought
them . . . to a state when they were long past coherent thought. So
Czechoslovakia was to be broken up.

The people came on to the streets, again in their thousands, but this
time weeping with grief, rage, shame and exhaustion. One morning I saw
a large number of men and women in the Old Square around the statue of
John Hus, burnt for his faith in 1415: they had been drawn there by a
common impulse yet they could say nothing, only sit there, their eyes
streaming, and their faces working.

> I. McDonald, *A Man of the Times*, Hamish Hamilton, 1976, pp.
> 32–8

Questions

a What did *The Times* article suggest to resolve the crisis?

b Why may this article have been published, and why was its effect so
considerable in Prague?

c How did many people in Prague react to the crisis?

d What does McDonald's eye-witness account add to textbook accounts of the Munich crisis?

* e How correct was it for Churchill to say in the Commons on 5
October that 'we have sustained a total and unmitigated defeat'?

* f Examine the validity and viability of the nation-state of Czechoslovakia (a) from 1918 to 1939, and (b) since the Second World War.

5 Opinions from Oxford and Cambridge

(a) So Baldwin passed from the scene, and Neville Chamberlain reigned
in his stead. He may not have had Baldwin's weakness for Fellows of All
Souls, but he was even more dependent on two of them. He wanted
Simon to succeed him as Chancellor of the Exchequer; while on his
breach with Eden – virtually a dismissal – Halifax came to his rescue and
became his Foreign Secretary. . . .

Chamberlain's course was hopeless from the start. It was at one time
the fashion to exonerate him and place most of the blame on Baldwin.

But where Baldwin's were sins of omission, Chamberlain's were sins of
10   deliberate commission. He really meant to come to terms with Hitler, to
make concession after concession to the man to buy an agreement. Apart
from the immorality of coming to terms with a criminal, it was always
sheer nonsense; for no agreement was possible except through submission
to Nazi Germany's domination of Europe and, with her allies and their
15   joint conquests, of the world . . . [In Simon's *Retrospect*, he says over
Czechoslovakia] 'Here was an intense strain in the centre of Europe
which, if it was not to lead from bad to worse, could only be relieved by a
concession.' There, in a sentence, is the whole psychological
misconception. It is no use making concessions to a blackmailer or an
20   aggressor; he will only ask for more. They were all taken back by Hitler's
march on Prague in March 1939, after the swag he had got, with their aid,
at Munich . . . . But why should they have been surprised?—as we have
seen, they had plenty of faithful warnings all along. And anyhow, what
are political leaders for? Do we employ them to fall for the enemies of
25   their country, to put across to us the lies they are such fools as to believe?
Not at all: the proper function of political leaders is precisely *not* to be
taken in, but to warn us. In fact, we were left without any effective means,
with no power whatever, in a hopeless minority, with no organs of
opinion at our command, to try and do something of what the
30   government should have been doing. We were all too ineffective,
condemned to making bricks without straw. . . .

Chamberlain knew no history . . . [and] had no conception of the
elementary necessity of keeping the balance of power on our side; no
conception of the Grand Alliance, or of its being the only way to contain
35   Hitler and keep Europe safe . . . .

The total upshot of [the appeasers'] efforts was to aid Nazi Germany to
achieve a position of brutal ascendancy, a threat to everybody else's
security or even existence, which only a war could end. This had the very
result of letting the Russians into the centre of Europe which the
40   appeasers . . . wished to prevent. Of course their responsibility was a
secondary one. The primary responsibility was all along that of the
Germans: the people in the strongest strategic position in Europe, the
keystone of the whole European system, but who never knew how to
behave, whether up or down, in the ascendant arrogant and brutal, in
45   defeat base and grovelling.

These men had no real conception of Germany's character or malign
record in modern history. Quite simply, we owe the wreck of Europe's
position in the world to Germany's total inability to play her proper rôle
in it.

A. L. Rowse, *All Souls and Appeasement*, Macmillan, 1961, pp.
57–9, 63, 117
50   (b)   **Pre-War German Policy**
Lord Grey's Views
The Way to Future Good Will

To the Editor of The Times

I agree . . . that Germany before the [First World] War 'had no
55 clear aims.' But I should be inclined to add that there were various
policies, some of them intransigent, some pacific, struggling against one
another, both in German public opinion and inside the German
government departments, and that the Kaiser was not good at the
difficult task of reconciling these opposites, partly because they were at
60 war inside his own mind. In July 1914, the military elements got the
upper hand in the fatal days. But that Austro-Hungarian action that
month was even more to blame than German is fully possible.

As regards 'predominance in Europe,' whether 'Germany wished' it or
not, she would have got it, if she had once more overrun France. And she
65 would have overrun France as well as Belgium if England had not
intervened. Then there would have been an end of the independence of all
Continental States in face of Germany, and in face of such a Europe
British independence could not have been maintained. German predominance would have been just as fatal to us whether it had been
70 intentionally or unintentionally acquired.

Such at least was Grey's view, and it will always be the view of many
Englishmen. But having said this, I welcome the main thesis of the
Baron's [Freiherr von Rheinbaben, former Secretary of State] letter, that
Germany and England must learn to 'tolerate,' though they cannot envy
75 or imitate, each other's form of government. Dictatorship and democracy must live side by side in peace, or civilization is doomed. For this
end I believe Englishmen would do well to remember that the Nazi form
of government is in large measure the outcome of Allied and British
injustice at Versailles in 1919. As to 1914 and the years before, I agree
80 with the Baron that Germans and English will seldom agree, the less so, I
would add, because of the egregious folly of the 'guilt' clause of the
Treaty of Versailles, which has acted, as might have been foreseen, as a
challenge to Germans to prove that their Government was not to blame
at all.

85   But the way to future good will does not lie in disputing about 1914.
Rather, as the Baron says, let us 'recognize and appreciate what is good
and what is great in other nation.'

Yours, &c.,

G.M. TREVELYAN

90 Hallington, Aug. 10.

Letter in The Times, 12 August 1937, p. 11.

Questions

a What does Rowse think were Chamberlain's main faults in foreign
affairs?

b What was 'the Grand Alliance' (line 34) and how does Rowse's use of
it reflect his study of history? Are there other examples of the use of
history?

c How does Trevelyan's emphasis for the responsibility of events in

Europe in the 1930s differ from that of Rowse? To what extent has the latter the advantage of hindsight?

d What do these extracts tell us about their authors' political views, and opinions about the role of Germany in Europe?

* e What post did Trevelyan hold when he wrote this letter, and what effect do you think his views might have had at the time?

* f Is there any reason to give greater credence to historians commenting on current affairs than to other people?

6 Revisionism

For ten years appeasement was the guiding philosophy of British foreign policy. From 1919 to 1929 successive British governments sought to influence European affairs in favour of an amelioration of tempers and an acceptance of discussions and negotiations as the best means of ensuring
5   peaceful change. That any change was necessary, France tended to deny. But British official opinion doubted whether a secure Europe could be based upon the Treaties of 1919, and had strong hopes of obtaining serious revision of those aspects of the Treaties that seemed to contain the seeds of future conflict. For ten years those hopes propelled policy
10 forward. Under the aegis of Lord Curzon, Ramsay MacDonald, and Austen Chamberlain important progress was made each year. Appeasement seemed not only morally justifiable, as being clearly preferable to rearmament, temper, and war, but also politically acceptable and diplomatically feasible.
15   The basis of appeasement was the acceptance of independent national states, each based as nearly as possible upon the Wilsonian principle of self-determination. With the disintegration in 1918 of the Russian, Turkish, German, and Habsburg Empires, the final stage had been reached in a process that had begun in Europe during the Napoleonic
20 wars – the evolution of strictly national as opposed to dynastic or strategic frontiers. Post-1918 diplomacy was geared to securing the final rectifications of frontiers still not conforming to this principle. Such frontiers were few. Most of them were the result of Versailles boundaries which had been drawn to the disadvantage of Germany. Thus there were
25 German-speaking people outside, but contiguous to the German frontier in Poland and Czechoslovakia, as well as Germans in Austria who had been forbidden union with Germany under Article 80 of the Treaty of Versailles. Even this clause was not irrevocable. According to the Treaty it could be altered 'with the consent of the Council of the League of
30 Nations'. Although France was unlikely to make such consent possible, the principle of making territorial adjustments was specifically and officially acknowledged.
        National 'inequalities' other than those of frontiers were also part of the Versailles Treaty, and were equally prone to the egalitarian touch of
35 appeasement. The disarmament of Germany, while France remained rearmed, was a German grievance which could be met either by

disarming France or allowing Germany to rearm. Both alternatives were considered by British policy-makers, and when the first proved impossible to secure, the second became logically difficult to resist.

40   A further 'inequality' was the exclusion of Germany from the League of Nations. British policy worked for Germany's inclusion, and looked forward to a time when the difference between 'Allied' and 'Enemy' powers, as embodied in the Versailles Treaty, would disappear, and cease to disturb and irritate Franco-German co-operation. In pursuing an
45   appeasement policy, the British Government sought to mediate between France and Germany. It was the policy of the 'honest broker'. Its aim was to allay mutual suspicions. It depended for its success upon both France and Germany realizing that it was a 'neutral' policy, designed to provide both countries with adequate security, under British patronage, and
50   thereby to make rearmament, military alliances, and war-plans unnecessary. The weakness of the policy was that France often felt that it was intended only to weaken her, and Germany that its aim was to keep her weak.

The policy of appeasement, as practised between 1919—29, was
55   wholly in Britain's interest. It was in no sense intended as an altruistic policy. British policy makers reasoned that the basis of European peace was a flourishing economic situation, unhampered by political bickerings, which, by ensuring general European prosperity, would also promote mutual understanding. Only by success in this policy could
60   Britain avoid becoming involved once again in a war rising out of European national ambitions and frustrations: a war which might well prove even more destructive of human life and social order than the 1914—18 war had been. . . .

But appeasement was never a coward's creed. It never signified retreat
65   or surrender from formal pledges. . . . Appeasement was not only an approach to foreign policy, it was a way of life, a method of human contact and progress. . . .

M. Gilbert, *The Roots of Appeasement*, Weidenfeld & Nicolson, 1966, pp. 96—7, 177

Questions

a   What cabinet position did Lord Curzon, Ramsay MacDonald and Austen Chamberlain (lines 10—11) hold in the period 1919—29?

b   What were 'the Wilsonian principle of self-determination' (lines 16—17) and 'the policy of the "honest broker"' (line 46)?

c   Outline the main aims of post-1918 diplomacy, and give examples of the difficulties in implementing these.

d   Why did Gilbert refer to 'the egalitarian touch of appeasement' (lines 34—5)? Why could France and Germany not always see appeasement in this light?

* e   When, if at all, did inter-war British foreign policy adopt 'a coward's creed' (line 64)?

* *f* Examine the impact of (a) Adolf Hitler and (b) Neville Chamberlain on the policy of appeasement in the 1930s.

Further Work

a Examine the view that appeasement was a noble and virtuous policy unsuited to dealing with a power like Nazi Germany.

b Attempt a defence of Chamberlain's foreign policy in 1938.

c What was the impact of the First World War on the views of the British public on foreign affairs between the wars?

d In 1934, Neville Chamberlain wrote that 'we cannot provide simultaneously for hostilities with Japan *and* Germany.' To what extent was appeasement a response to Britain's wider problems of imperial responsibility, in which Europe took second place?

e Can the philosophy of appeasement be identified in any major European or world crisis since 1945?

f Attempting counter-factual analysis, would it have been preferable for Britain and France if war with Germany had broken out in 1936 or 1938?

VIII 'A New Jerusalem'? — the Labour Government and Social Reform 1945—51

Introduction

In 1940 an American journalist writing for the *New York Herald Tribune* commented that 'Hitler is doing what centuries of English history have not accomplished — he is breaking down the class structure of England'. A. J. P. Taylor saw the Second World War as 'a brief period in which the English people felt they belonged to a truly democratic community'. Long before victory was in sight all sections of society began thinking about the post-war world, dreaming of a new order quite different from the old. Out of total war and all its horrors enormous hope was born and the idea of a 'New Jerusalem' conceived. This chapter is concerned with how the Labour Government from 1945 to 1951 attempted to implement radical social reform and about the opposition to this development from the Conservative Party.

This new optimism can be traced back to the publication of the Beveridge Report in November 1942 which almost coincided with the Allied victory at El Alamein. The first symbolised the idealism of social reconstruction while the latter was seen as the beginning of total victory. There was unanimous agreement about two things. First, that there should should be no repetition of the fiasco which followed 1918 — a nightmare of slump, unemployment and distress. Secondly, a set of very basic requirements was laid down: work for all, social security, a right to a decent standard of living, and genuine international cooperation. It was not just Labour, but Liberal and even Tory supporters who were behind this desire for change and reform. It is significant that the inventor of the term 'Welfare State' was that pillar of the Establishment, the Archbishop of Canterbury, William Temple.

Most observers expected the Conservatives to win the General Election in 1945. Stalin told Churchill at the Potsdam Conference that his sources indicated a Tory majority of eighty. But during the war there had been a strong movement to the Labour Party which could be detected in both by-elections and opinion polls. Yet *The Times* found 'nothing remarkable' in the Conservatives losing Chelmsford and Motherwell in April 1945. The results totally confounded most observers. Labour won with an absolute majority of a massive 154. In every area of the country Labour swept to victory and the size of the national swing towards it was 12 per cent. The confidence and the determination of Labour to act after this electoral success can be seen in the phrase 'We are the masters now!', shouted, it is said, by a Labour MP during a debate in 1946.

Between 1945 and 1951 the Labour Government undertook a programme of massive reform. It has been called 'the quiet' or 'the peaceful revolution'. Just how far this is a valid description is debatable. Whether the reforms were revolutionary or evolutionary is an issue which needs consideration. The debate which is shown in the manifestos was not about whether a Welfare State was needed, it was about the means by which it would be achieved. The issues of individualism versus collectivism, central control versus local control, competition versus cooperation, and reality and illusion can all be identified. The degree of success which the historian ascribes to these reforms depends on what he sees as 'the Welfare State'. As Bédarida argues, there are at least three possible meanings for this enigmatic concept.

No one would doubt that the achievements of the Labour governments were considerable. They undertook the massive task of social reconstruction and social transformation with vigour and attempted to establish a new social order. Yet their success in this area must be viewed against their economic failures and inept foreign policy. The creation of the Welfare State did not, really, involve a transformation of society. It was, to a considerable degree, a substitute for it.

Further Reading

There are many surveys of the post-1945 period, but these will be found most useful:

C. J. Bartlett, *A History of Postwar Britain 1945–74* (Longman, 1977)

P. Calvocoressi, *The British Experience 1945–75* (Penguin, 1979), a well-written, witty book.

L. J. Macfarlane, *Issues in British Politics since 1945* (Longman, 1975), one of the Political Realities series.

L. A. Monk, *Britain 1945–1970* (Bell, 1976).

A. Sked and C. Cook, *Post-War Britain: a Political History* (Penguin 1979), perhaps the best introduction.

The important themes in post-war politics are pursued in

C. Cook and J. Ramsden (eds), *Trends in British Politics* (Macmillan, 1978).

On the Labour Party during this period the following are essential reading:

P. Adelman, *The Rise of the Labour Party 1880–1945* (Longman, 1972), one of the excellent Seminar Studies in History series.

C. Cook and I. Taylor (eds), *The Labour Party: an introduction to its history, structure and politics* (Longman 1980), especially the chapter by David Steel.

M. Sissons (ed.), *The Age of Austerity* (London 1963), essays on the post-war Labour Government.

H. Pelling, *A Short History of the Labour Party* (Macmillan, 1976)

P. Addison, *The Road to 1945* (London, 1975), provides interesting insights on the period after 1945.

This period can also be approached through biography:

A. Bullock, *The Life and Times of Ernest Bevin* (2 vols, 1960–67)

M. Foot, *Aneurin Bevan*, (2 vols, 1962–73)

P. Williams, *Hugh Gaitskell* (London, 1979)

It is unfortunate that there is still no satisfactory biography of Clement Attlee.

For more details on social policy during this period see the following:

R. C. Birch, *The Shaping of the Welfare State* (Longman, 1974, one of the Seminar Studies in History series)

D. Fraser, *The Evolution of the British Welfare State* (Macmillan, 1973), places the development of social policy in its historical perspective.

T. H. Marshall, *Social Policy* (London, 1972), an excellent and lucid survey.

J. F. Sleeman, *The Welfare State: its aims, benefits and costs* (London, 1973)

R. M. Titmuss, *Essays on the Welfare State* (London, 1958), a good sample by perhaps the most influential thinker on the Welfare State.

Good biographies of the master-minds of the Welfare State can also be found:

J. F. Harris, *Beveridge* (Oxford, 1979) probably the definitive biography.

D. E. Moggridge, *Keynes* (Fontana, 1976), the best starting point on his ideas, and has the advantage of being brief.

1   The Principles Stated – Beveridge, 1942

6   In proceeding from this first comprehensive survey of social insurance to the next task—of making recommendations—three guiding principles may be laid down at the outset.

7   The first principle is that any proposals for the future, while they
5   should use to the full the experience gathered in the past, should not be restricted by consideration of sectional interests established in the obtaining of that experience. Now, when the war is abolishing landmarks of every kind, is the opportunity for using experience in a clear field. A revolutionary moment in the world's history is a time for revolutions,
10   not patching.

8   The second principle is that organization of social insurance should be treated as one part only of a comprehensive policy of social progress. Social insurance fully developed may provide income security; it is an attack upon Want. But Want is only one of the five giants on the road of
15   reconstruction and in some ways the easiest to attack. The others are Disease, Ignorance, Squalor and Idleness.

9   The third principle is that social security must be achieved by co-operation between the State and the individual. The State should offer security for service and contribution. The State in organising security
20   should not stifle incentive, opportunity, responsibility; in establishing a national minimum, it should leave room and encouragement for voluntary action by each individual to provide more than that minimum for himself and his family.

10   The Plan for Social Security set out in this Report is built upon these
25   principles. It uses experience but is not tied to experience. It is put forward
as a limited contribution to a wider social policy. . . . It is, first and
foremost, a plan of insurance – of giving in return for contributions
benefits up to subsistence level, as of right and without means tests, so that
individuals may build freely upon it.

> Social Insurance and Allied Services (Cmd 6404) – the Beveridge
> Report – presented to Parliament, November 1942, HMSO pp.
> 6–7

Questions

a   (i) What do 'social insurance' (line 1), 'subsistence level' (line 28) and
'means test' (line 28) mean and why were they important to the
Beveridge Report?
(ii) Who were the 'sectional interests established in the obtaining of
that experience' (lines 6–7)? What was their reaction to the Report?
(iii) What were 'the five Giants' (lines 14–16)? In what ways was
each a problem in the period up to 1942?
* b   Who was Sir William Beveridge and what part had he played in the
development of social policies since 1908?
c   What were the three principles upon which the Report was based? Do
you think that Beveridge identified the correct principles?
* d   How much was Beveridge's perspective of social policy in 1942
influenced by developments since 1908? Did this create problems for
the development of the Welfare State?
* e   How revolutionary was the Beveridge Report?
* f   The Beveridge Report is an excellent example of patching. Do you
agree?

2   Social Policy 1945–51 – the Establishment of the Welfare State?

A THE MANIFESTOS

CONSERVATIVE MANIFESTO 1945
This is the time for freeing energies, not stifling them. Britain's greatness
has been built on character and daring, not on docility to a State Machine.
At all costs we must preserve that spirit and independence and that 'Right
to live by no man's leave underneath the law'. . . .

5   *National Insurance*

National wellbeing is founded on good employment, good housing and
good health. But there always remain those personal hazards of fortune,
such as illness, accident or loss of a job, or industrial injury, which may
leave the individual and his family unexpectedly in distress. In addition,
10   old age, death and child-birth throw heavy burdens upon the family
income.

One of our most important tasks will be to pass into law and bring into action as soon as we can a nation-wide and compulsory scheme of National Insurance based on the plan announced by the Government of all Parties in 1944. . . .

The scheme will not justify itself to the public unless the service given to them in return for their contributions combines human understanding with efficiency. There must be no queuing up for sickness benefits by those who are entitled to them. The same standard of intimacy in personal relationships must be maintained as formerly.

Health

The health services of the country will be made available to all citizens. Everyone will contribute to the cost, and no one will be denied the attention, the treatment or the appliances he requires because he cannot afford them.

We propose to create a comprehensive health service covering the whole range of medical treatment from the general practitioner to the specialist. . . .

At the same time Medicine will be left free to develop along its own lines, and to achieve preventive as well as curative triumphs. Liberty is an essential condition of scientific progress. . . .

Education

The Education Act set forth in the 'Four Years' Plan' has already been piloted through Parliament by Mr Butler. Our task in the coming years will be to remodel our educational system according to the new law. . . . Our object is to provide education which will not produce a standardised or utility child, useful only as a cog in a nationalised and bureaucratic machine, but will enable the child to develop his or her responsible place, first in the world of school, and then as a citizen. . . .

We are dedicated to the purpose of helping to rebuild Britain on the sure foundations on which her greatness rests. In recent generations, enormous material progress has been made. That progress must be extended and accelerated not by subordinating the individual to the authority of the State, but by providing the conditions in which no one shall be precluded by poverty, ignorance, insecurity, or the selfishness of others from making the best of the gifts which Providence has endowed him.

Our programme is not based upon unproved theories or fine phrases, but upon principles that have been tested anew in the fires of war and not found wanting. . . .

in F. W. S. Craig (ed.) *British General Election Manifestos 1900– 1974*, Macmillan, 1975, pp. 113, 117–19, 122–3

LET US FACE THE FUTURE — LABOUR MANIFESTO 1945

The nation wants food, work and homes. It wants more than that — it wants good food in plenty, useful work for all, and comfortable, labour-

saving homes that take full advantage of the resources of modern science
and productive industry. It wants a high and rising standard of living,
5   security for all against a rainy day, an educational system that will give
every boy and girl a chance to develop the best that is in them.

Houses and the Building Programme

Everyone says that we must have houses. Only the Labour Party is ready
to take the necessary steps – a full programme of land planning and
10   drastic action to ensure an efficient building industry that will neither
burden the community with a crippling financial load nor impose bad
conditions and heavy unemployment on its workpeople. . . . Housing
will be one of the greatest and one of the earliest tests of a Government's
real determination to put the nation first. Labour's pledge is firm and
15   direct – it will proceed with a housing programme with the maximum
practical speed until every family in this island has a good standard of
accommodation. That may well mean centralised purchasing and
pooling of building materials and components by the State, together with
price control. . . .

20   *Education and Recreation*

An important step forward has been taken by the passing of the recent
Education Act. Labour will put that Act not merely into legal force but
into practical effect, including the raising of the school leaving age to 16 at
the earliest possible moment, 'further' or adult education, and free
25   secondary education for all. . . . National and local authorities should
co-operate to enable people to enjoy their leisure to the full, to have
opportunities for healthy recreation. . . .

Health of the Nation and its Children

Money must no longer be the passport to the best treatment.
30   In the new National Health Service there should be health centres
where the people may get the best that modern science can offer, more
and better hospitals, and proper conditions for our doctors and
nurses. . . .

Social Insurance Against the Rainy Day

35   The Labour Party has played a leading part in the long campaign for
proper social security for all – social provision against rainy days,
coupled with economic policies calculated to reduce rainy days to a
minimum. Labour led the fight against the mean and shabby treatment
which was the lot of millions while Conservative Governments were in
40   power over long years. A Labour Government will press on rapidly with
legislation extending social insurance over the necessary wide field to all.
    But great national programmes of education, health and social services
are costly things. Only an efficient and prosperous nation can afford them
in full measure. If, unhappily, bad times were to come, and our opponents
45   were in power, then, running true to form, they would be likely to cut
these social provisions on the plea that the nation could not meet the cost.

That was the line they adopted on at least three occasions between the
wars.

50   There is no good reason why Britain should not afford such
programmes, but she will need full employment and the highest possible
industrial efficiency in order to do so. . . .

   . . . the effective choice of the people in this Election will be between
the Conservative Party, standing for the protection of the 'rights' of
private economic interest, and the Labour Party, allied with the great
55 Trade Union and co-operative Movements, standing for wise organization and the use of the economic assets of the nation for the public
good. . . .

             ibid. pp. 124, 128−30, 131

THIS IS THE ROAD − CONSERVATIVE MANIFESTO 1950
The Socialist Failure

But the Socialists have failed in their duty. National resources have been
squandered. Individual effort has been discouraged or suppressed.
National unity has been deeply injured. The Government have shrunk
5 from the realities of the situation and have not told the people the truth.

The Socialist Deception

From the time they acquired power they pretended that their policy was
bringing the prosperity they promised. . . . They spread the tale that
social welfare is something to be had from the State free, gratis and for
10 nothing. They have put more money into circulation, but it has bought
less and less. . . .

Socialist Mismanagement

   . . . Socialism has imposed a crushing burden of taxation amounting to
eight shillings of every pound earned in this country. Enterprise and extra
15 effort has been stifled. Success has been penalised. Thrift and savings have
been discouraged. A vote for Socialism is a vote to continue the policy
which has endangered our present economic independence both as a
nation and as men and women. . . .

   The Social Services were born of Parliaments with Conservative and
20 Liberal majorities. They rest on the productive effort of British industry
and agriculture. The Socialists have by inflation reduced their value and
compromised their future. By energetic action they can be saved and
their value maintained. Britain can only enjoy the social services for
which she is prepared to work.

25   We are determined to give a solid base of social security below which
none shall fall and above which each must be encouraged to rise to the
utmost limit of his ability. . . .

Property-owning Democracy

We intend to help all those who wish to own a house of their own or a
30 small holding. A true property-owning democracy must be based upon

the wide distribution of private housing, not upon its absorption in the State machine.

Housing

35 Upon good housing depends the health and happiness of every family. Before the war, under free enterprise with a Conservative government, the nation was getting a thousand new houses every day. The latest Socialist target is five hundred. . . . We shall revive the confidence of the Building Industry and greatly widen the scope for the independent builder. . . .

40 *The Health Service*

We pledge ourselves to maintain and improve the Health Service. Every year the Estimates laid before Parliament have been greatly exceeded. Administrative efficiency and correct priorities throughout the whole system must be assured, so that the proper balance is maintained and the
45 hardest needs met first. . . .

Pensions

(a) War Pensions
War Pensions have been affected by the reduced purchasing power of money. We shall set up a Select Committee to see what improvements
50 should be made, having regard to national resources.
(b) Contributory and Non-Contributory Pensions
There are a number of improvements which ought to be made –
An increase in the limit of weekly earnings without reduction of pensions from 30s. to 45s. in the case of widows with children and 20s.
55 to 30s. for women pensioners with dependants.

Assessments of casual earnings of old age pensioners on a monthly instead of a weekly basis.

Revision of the assumed rates of interest on capital saved by applicants for non-contributory pensions

> ibid. pp. 139– 40, 146–9

LET US WIN THROUGH TOGETHER – LABOUR MANIFESTO 1950

The task now is to carry the nation through to complete recovery. And that will mean continued, mighty efforts from us all. The choice for the electors is between the Labour Party – the party of positive action, of constructive progress, the true party of the nation – and the Conservat-
5 ive Party – the party of outdated ideas, of unemployment, of privilege.

The New Moral Order

Socialism is not bread alone. Economic security and freedom from the enslaving material bonds of capitalism are not the final goals. They are means to the greater end – the evolution of a people more kindly,
10 intelligent, free, co-operative, enterprising and rich in culture. They are

the means to the greater end of the full and free development of every individual person. . . . We believe that all citizens have obligations to fulfil as well as rights to enjoy. . . .

Helping Each Other in Time of Need

15 Labour has honoured the pledge it made in 1945 to make social security the birthright of every citizen. Today destitution has been banished. The best medical care is available to everybody in the land.

Great Acts of Parliament — the National Insurance, Industrial Injuries, National Assistance and National Health Services Acts — have been
20 placed on the Statute Book. This social legislation has benefited all sections of the community, including members of the middle classes. Hundreds of thousands of middle class and professional families have been relieved of one of their worst anxieties — the fear of sudden illness, the expensive operation, the doctors' crippling bills. What is needed now
25 is not so much new legislation as the wise development, through efficient and economical administration, of the services provided by these Acts. . . .

  ibid. pp. 152–3, 158

CONSERVATIVE MANIFESTO 1951

Contrast our position today with what it was six years ago. Then all our foes had yielded. We all had the right to believe and hope that the fear of war would not afflict our generation nor our children. . . . We were a united people at home, and it was only by being united that we had
5 survived the deadly perils through which we had come and had kept the flag of freedom flying. . . . The attempt to impose a doctrinaire Socialism upon an Island which had grown great and famous by free enterprise has inflicted serious injury upon our strength and prosperity. . . .
10 Housing is the first of the social services. It is also one of the keys to increased productivity. Work, family life, health and education are all undermined by overcrowded homes. Therefore a Conservative and Unionist Government will give housing a priority second only to defence. Our target remains 300,000 houses a year. There should be no
15 reduction in the number of houses and flats built to let but more freedom must be given to the private builder. In a property-owning democracy, the more people who own their homes the better.

In Education and in Health some of the most crying needs are not being met. For the money now being spent we will provide better services and
20 so fulfil the high hopes we all held when we planned the improvements during the war. . . .

We shall review the position of pensioners, including war pensioners, and see that the hardest needs are met first. The care and comfort of the elderly is a sacred trust. Some of them prefer to remain at work and there
25 must be encouragement for them to do so. . . .

  ibid. pp. 169, 172

Labour – proud of its record, sure in its policies – confidently asks the electors to renew its mandate.

5   Four main tasks face our nation: to secure peace; to maintain full employment and increase productivity; to bring down the cost of living; to build a just society. Only with a Labour Government can the British people achieve these aims. . . .

Social Justice

Contrast Britain in the inter-war years with Britain today. Then we had mass unemployment; mass fear; mass misery. Now we have full
10   employment.

Then millions suffered from insecurity and want. Now we have social security for every man, woman and child.

Then dread of doctors' bills was a nightmare in countless homes so that good health cost more than most people could afford to pay. Now we
15   have a national health scheme which is the admiration of the post-war world.

Then we had the workhouse and the Poor Law for the old people. Now we have a national insurance system covering the whole population with greatly improved pensions and a humane National Assistance
20   scheme.

Then only 39 per cent of the nation's personal incomes after taxation went to the wage earner, and 34 per cent to rent, interest and profit. Now, following Labour's great reforms in taxation, 48 per cent goes in wages and only 25 per cent in rent, interest and profit.

25   There has, indeed, been progress, but much more remains to be done in the redistribution of income and of property to ensure that those who create the nation's wealth receive their just reward. Half of Britain's wealth is still owned by 1 per cent of the population.

The Tories are against a more equal society. They stand as they have
30   always stood, for privilege. In Parliament they proposed cuts in taxation on large incomes and fought for profits tax. They opposed the dividends freeze. . . . They have voted in Parliament against the National Health Service, and they condemned the Labour Government for being 'too hasty' in introducing family allowances and raising old age pensions. . . .

        ibid pp. 173, 175–6

B THE RESULTS

	Total votes	MPs elected	Candidates	% share of total votes
1945, Thursday 5 July				
Conservative	9 988 306	213	624	40.1
Liberal	2 248 226	12	306	18.6
Labour	11 995 152	293	604	50.4
Communist	102 780	2	21	12.7

Common				
Wealth	110 634	1	23	12.6
Others	640 880	19	104	15.4
Turnout 72.7%	25 085 978	640	1682	

1950, Thursday 23 February
Conservative	12 502 567	298	620	43.7
Liberal	2 621 548	9	475	11.8
Labour	13 266 592	315	617	46.7
Communist	91 746	—	100	2.0
Others	290 218	3	56	12.6
Turnout 84%	—	625	1868	

1951, Thursday 25 October
Conservative	13 717 538	321	617	48.6
Liberal	730 556	6	109	14.7
Labour	13 948 605	295	617	49.2
Communist	21 640	—	10	4.4
Others	177 329	3	23	16.8
Turnout 82.5%	—	625	1376	

D. Butler and A. Sloman *British Political Facts 1900—1975*, Macmillan, 1975, p. 184.

C THE POLLS

The British Institute of Public Opinion was founded in 1937. Its name was changed in 1952 to Social Surveys (Gallup Poll) Ltd. The following tables show in summary form the answers to the question, 'If there were a General Election tomorrow, how would you vote?'

		Con %	Lab %	Lib %	Others %	Don't know	Con lead over Lab %
1946	Jan	30	49	10	4	7	−19
	May	37	40	12	3	8	−3
1947	Jan	38	41	11	2	8	−3
	Mar	38	38	9	2	13	0
	Jul	38	38	11	2	11	0
	Nov	44	33	8	2	13	11
1948	Jan	38	37	9	1	15	1
	Mar	38	36	7	2	17	2
	Jul	42	35	8	3	12	7
	Nov	38	36	7	2	17	2
1949	Jan	38	35	11	2	14	3
	Mar	36	36	11	2	14	−1
	Jul	38	36	10	2	14	3
	Nov	40	32	11	1	16	8
1950	Jan	38	38	10	2	12	0
	Mar	41	43	6	1	9	−2
	Jul	38	39	10	3	10	−1
	Oct	40	42	9	0	10	−2

1951	Jan	44	33	9	1	13	11
	Mar	44	33	8	1	14	11
	Jul	43	34	9	1	13	9
	Oct	45	39	5	0	11	6

ibid, pp. 204–5.

Questions

The aim of this section of work on social policy between 1945 and 1951 is to see how far certain kinds of evidence can be 'squeezed'.

a   What problems does the historian have to face when dealing with manifestos, election results and opinion polls in this period?

b   Using only the material available, examine the success of Labour's social policies between 1945 and 1951. How successful was Conservative opposition to it?

c   Compare the party images (self-image and image of the other party) contained in the manifestos.

d   What tactics do the Conservatives employ in their manifestos to try to discredit the Labour Party and its policies?

*   e   Is there any relationship between party manifestos and election results?

*   f   What other sources of information could the historian of social policy use to elucidate the character of change in this period?

*   g   Conservative and Labour parties both agreed over the need for a comprehensive social policy after the war. All they disagreed about was the means. Discuss.

3   The Perspective of Time

They [the Labour government elected in 1945] had started with boundless ambition. They had envisaged a total transformation of society, but they were only able to fulfil a fraction of their programme, namely the achievement of what came to be known as the Welfare State,
5   i.e. a new social set-up that guaranteed a minimum of security and benefit to all. The expression soon acquired official status, appearing in the Oxford English Dictionary as early as 1955 as 'a polity so organised that every member of the community is assured of his due maintenance with the most advantageous conditions possible for all'. It is open to two
10   definitions. For a rather narrow interpretation one may take the five points enunciated by M. Bruce (*The Coming of the Welfare State*). . . . (1) to guarantee to everyone. . . a decent standard of living, without this minimum income being necessarily earned through employment (thanks to the dual notion of insurance and assistance); (2) to protect everyone
15   against the vicissitudes of daily life (illness, unemployment etc.); (3) to help family life develop and thrive (hence family allowances); (4) to treat health and education as public services. . . . ; (5) to develop and improve all public establishments and equipment that may conduce to the

betterment of personal life (housing, the environment, leisure activities).
Seen in this light, the Welfare State appears as the end-product of a long
history, its origins far back in the past. . . .

But this is a narrow, rather technical definition . . . amounting to little
more than an enlargement of the social services. The phrase may be
allowed a rather wider sense. In this it stands as the symbol of the structure
of post-war Britain – a society with a mixed economy and full
employment, where individualism is tempered by State intervention,
where the right to work and a basic standard of living are guaranteed, and
the working-class movement, now accepted and recognized, finds its
rightful place in the nation.

By its own admission Labour's 'revolution' must be seen in the
perspective of 'evolution'. The key word is 'social justice'. Without in the
least denying the collectivist principles inscribed on Labour's tablets, the
revolution found its main inspiration in two Liberals: first Beveridge,
then Keynes. These were the two masterminds whose ideas guided
Labour's actions. . . .

In seeking to determine the significance of the Welfare State one must
bear three points in mind. Firstly, to use the word 'revolution' is to
devalue its meaning. . . . In the second place, the arrival of the Welfare
State was situated in the mainstream of the history of democratic
freedom, linking the pioneers of the London Corresponding Society with
the militants of the Independent Labour Party, the Benthamites, with the
Fabians, the Nonconformist conscience with Christian
Socialism. . . . Finally, if the Welfare State was the grandchild of
Beveridge and Keynes, it was no less the child of the Fabians, since it
concentrated on legislative, administrative and centralizing methods to
the detriment of 'workers' control'. But in thus stamping on any frail
aspiration towards a libertarian organization of society, Labour laid itself
open to a charge that would weigh heavily on it in the future, namely that
of wanting to impose a bureaucratic form of socialism. . . .

F. Bédarida, *A Social History of England 1851—1975*, Methuen,
1979, pp. 191—2, 195—6

Questions

a   (i) Who were Beveridge and Keynes (lines 33—4)?
    (ii) What are 'mixed economy and full employment' (lines 25—6)?
    (iii) Who were 'the Fabians' (line 42) and what significance did they
have for the Labour Party?
    (iv) Explain why the Labour governments from 1945—51 were
'only able to fulfil a fraction of their programme' (line 3)?
    (v) Explain 'the dual notion of insurance and assistance' (line 14)
    (vi) How valid is the assertion contained in lines 20—21?
b   What are the three definitions of the Welfare State contained in the
passage? Which do you find the most convincing and why?
c   What three points must one bear in mind when attempting to
determine the significance of the Welfare State?

* *d* The Welfare State necessitated a bureaucratic form of socialism. This led to the collectivist rather than democratic tradition in the Labour Movement triumphing. Why was this important?

* *e* The problem of definition is the major difficulty facing the historian. Do you agree?

Further Work

a Why did the Labour Party win the 1945 and 1950 General Elections and lose the 1951 Election?

b What role did personality play in the development of Labour Party policy between 1945 and 1951?

c Have social welfare policies in the twentieth century been evolutionary in development?

d The Labour Party may have dealt effectively with the question of social reform but they were largely unsuccessful in other areas of domestic policy. Discuss.

e The tensions between individualism and collectivism can be seen at their most pronounced between 1945 and 1951. Examine this issue with reference to both Labour and Conservative parties.

f Did the 1945–51 period see the emergence of the mass media as a major political force?

g Compare and contrast Churchill and Attlee as leaders of their respective parties.

IX   Winds of Change

Introduction

The British presence in India was often represented as the jewel in the Imperial crown, and yet even in the late nineteenth century Gladstone had perceived the problem that was not resolved until 1947: 'The truth as to India cannot too soon be understood. There are two policies, fundamentally different. . . . One of them treats India as a child treats a doll, and defends it against other children; the other places all its hopes for the permanence of our Indian rule in our good government of India. . . . Let us only make common cause with her people: let them feel that we are there to give more than we receive.'

Successive governments proved unwilling to tackle the problem effectively, and the growth of opposition like Gandhi's Congress Party with its campaigns of civil disobedience was met with hostility (including the notorious Amritsar massacre of 1919), especially from Conservatives like Churchill. Despite appalling suffering the transition to dominion status in 1947 was achieved with remarkable speed, largely due to the personal qualities of the last viceroy, Viscount Mountbatten of Burma. The passing of the Raj ended not only several centuries of British rule but also closed many avenues of training, expertise and adventure for diplomats and soldiers who developed India and their own characters in one of the most exacting and rewarding training-grounds. (The last sentence is, in itself, an interesting statement on how the Empire may be viewed in retrospect!)

The Suez Crisis of 1956 was 'the last dying convulsion of British Imperialism' as Anthony Nutting described it. The Conservative Prime Minister, Anthony Eden, was convinced that Europe was reliving the 1930s and saw in Colonel Nasser another Mussolini. Hugh Thomas thought that Eden 'saw Egypt through a forest of Flanders poppies and gleaming jackboots.' The result was a *débâcle* in which British public opinion was as divided as in 1938, which saw the nadir of Anglo-American relations, and the downfall of Eden himself. Controversy still exists over the extent to which Britain and France were in collusion with Israel on the war between Israel and Egypt. In view of subsequent Arab-Israeli crises and wars, the Suez War of 1956 is receding in importance, but it shows clearly how difficult it is for politicians to attempt to learn definite lessons from history.

The perspective of the 1980s enables us to see the impossibility of withstanding the forces of nationalism in India, Egypt and elsewhere, when nationalism had been accepted in Europe in the nineteenth or early twentieth centuries. It is also salutary for historians of the British Empire to see the problem from 'the other side' as a reading of Mrs Pandit's book offers.

Further Reading

INDIA

C. Cross, *The Fall of the British Empire, 1918–1968* (Hodder and Stoughton, 1968), a very useful survey of the problems of the Empire in the twentieth century; particularly good on India.

R. Kipling, *Kim* (Macmillan, 1901) an enjoyable insight into the British impact on India by its greatest exponent.

Earl Mountbatten of Burma, *Reflections on the Transfer of Power and Jawaharlal Nehru* (Cambridge UP, 1968), a lecture on the events of 1947 with very useful comments and anecdotes.

V. L. Pandit, *The Scope of Happiness* (Weidenfeld and Nicolson, 1979), a beautifully written personal memoir of the struggle for independence in India and the problems of the new nation, by Nehru's sister.

B. Porter, *The Lion's Share: A Short History of British Imperialism, 1850–1970* (Longman, 1975), a good guide to the main events and interpretations.

SUEZ

A. J. Barker, *Suez: The Seven Day War* (Faber and Faber, 1964), a readable military account.

L. D. Epstein, *British Politics in the Suez Crisis* (Pall Mall, 1964), an insight into the effects of Suez on the political parties.

Selwyn Lloyd, *Suez 1956* (Jonathan Cape, 1978), the author was a key participant but his book sheds little light on the secret talks.

H. Thomas, *The Suez Affair* (Weidenfeld and Nicolson, 1966–7), an expanded version of articles in *The Sunday Times*, with useful comments on the crisis from a wide perspective.

1 A Young Man's View of British India

I more or less drifted towards India and when I had passed that formidable examination of 15 three-hour papers, as it was then, there was no going back. . . . It was all so unattractive in that Madras hotel, the heat, the harsh light, the mosquito nets, those abominable wicker chaises-
5 longues . . . the electric fans scattering the papers, the air of hopelessness of the emaciated figures sweeping the verandahs. I felt myself enveloped in a debilitating lassitude and asked myself over and over again: Why had I come? Was this to be my whole life?

I was met with immediate kindness, being removed from the hotel to
10 the house of a senior English member of the Madras secretariat, but that

only increased my depression. My hosts were so kind, but they belonged
to and were obviously happy in this strange world, for which I could feel
no sympathy. I soon realized that there were separate societies, British and
Indian, which only mixed on an official plane. I was put up for the Madras
15 Club, which no Indian might penetrate, however distinguished in the
British service, save the horde of servants in their white linen hats and
swirling skirts. . . .

Custom required that I should drive round the houses of the mandarins
of the civil service in the heat of the day, pushing my visiting cards
20 through the slits in the boxes to be found at every gate. . . . As I went
round and round, I ruminated on my new social surroundings. . . . It
was not just the question of club membership . . . it was the unnatural
association of a rigidly closed community of British civil servants at the
top, then the soldiers and lastly the 'box wallahs' that is, the merchants
25 and industrialists but not the retailers, who didn't qualify . . . and an as
rigidly closed community of Indians, or rather a number of mutually
exclusive Indian communities based on caste, each side being members of
the 'establishment' for official purposes, but neither wanting to assimilate
themselves to the other by varying their own customs and beliefs, or
30 wanting to have too much to do with the other outside the office and
official functions. . . . Neither side made any real effort to get out of the
strait-jacket of conflicting backgrounds and if the British were most at
fault in their feeling of belonging to a superior race, they had looking-
glass logic on their side, for if they were not superior, what were they
35 doing in India anyway? . . .

Then, suddenly, I was sent for a few months to Ootacamund, the
famous hill station in the Nilgiri hills . . . the downs were . . . bare hills
of great beauty, furnished only with clumps of indigenous trees and the
bee-hive huts of the Todas, the earliest known inhabitants of the hill who
40 still lived there. . . . Ootacamund was a typical English county
community, with the Ooty hounds, the race course and golf course, the
shooting and fishing and amateur theatricals, peopled by government
officials up for the summer complete with clerks and files, and coffee and
tea planters from the country around who lived a hard, open air life for 51
45 weeks of the year and remained happily drunk throughout the fifty-
second, known as planters' week.

A thousand miles away the civil disobedience movement was raging as
Gandhi led his famous 'salt-march', but the echoes of it penetrated only
fitfully to the distant refuge in the hills. . . .
50 [Back in Madras] I stayed for a time with the Chief Secretary who
lived in a splendid house. . . . In the morning [he] would appear on the
top step of the fine staircase . . . dressed . . . in silk suit, Old Etonian tie
and furry white topee. A petition would be handed to him. He would
adjust his monocle, glance at it and hand it to his servant who had
55 probably been paid one rupee by the petitioner and who would perhaps
recommend that the petition be sent to the Board of Revenue. It was a
totally irregular procedure, but satisfied everybody, for it represented
personal contact between Government and subject. . . .

I had learnt . . . that the unnatural relations between British and
60 Indian sprang from history and that the time was coming when the
British ought to leave if they could succeed in disentangling themselves
without leaving intolerable strife behind. Meanwhile, I could understand
the strength of Indian nationalism and at the same time applaud the
loyalty of Indians in the employment of the British to the service which
65 they had accepted as their career, against all the weight of nationalist
opinion. In the old phrase, they were true to their salt. There was, I
recognized, much that was good in Indian life, and though social reform
was badly needed, it could not go far under the British. It needed the
impulse which could only be given by an Indian government. The British
70 had planted a democratic system, but had buttressed it with traditional
Indian autocracy. The Indians would have to find their own way ahead.
   H. Trevelyan, *Public and Private*, Hamish Hamilton, 1980,
   pp. 3–4, 6–7, 10–12

Questions

a Why would new arrivals in India find aspects of it 'so unattractive'
   (line 3)?
b Explain 'mandarins of the civil service' (lines 18–19); 'hill station'
   (line 37); 'The civil disobedience movement' (line 47). How may this
   account be roughly dated?
c What was the nature of the British class and Indian caste systems?
   Were features of English upper-class life evident in India?
d Examine the vices and virtues of the British presence in India
   contained in this memoir.
* e Why was it becoming necessary for the British to leave India by the
   1930s? What motivated the men who entered the Indian Civil
   Service between the wars?
* f What comparable fields of experience are available today for young
   men like Humphrey Trevelyan?

2   Indian Involvement

In 1935 the British Parliament passed the Government of India Act, 1935,
introducing provincial autonomy. This act envisaged responsible government in provincial legislatures but reserved the right of the Centre, the
federal government, in New Delhi, to have charge of defence, foreign
5 affairs, tribal areas . . . [and] also retained representation on a communal
basis. . . .
   Once the decision to contest the elections was arrived at, the election
manifesto was prepared. This . . . rejected the Government of India Act
but resolved to continue the national struggle and resist imperialism by
10 entering the legislatures. . . . This policy was to end exploitation of the
masses, and . . . to work for a constitution that would grant each

citizen . . . the right of free expression of opinion and association, freedom of conscience, the protection of cultural and minority rights, equality before the law irrespective of caste, creed, or sex, and many other rights that were later incorporated in the Constitution of free India . . . 1950. A committee in each province selected the Congress candidates. . . . Ranjit and I were both offered tickets and accepted them. . . . The problem . . . was one of finances. The other side . . . were mostly big landowners, princelings, and supporters of the status quo. They lacked neither money nor support from their British masters. In the balance, however, Congress had a large section of the country behind it. . . . Ranjit's opponent was the Raja of Manda, a . . . (landowner) of the district. Mine . . . was Lady Srivastava, the wife of the Education Member in the Viceroy's Council. . . .

Polling day drew near, and since it was impossible for us to compete with those who were opposing us in the matter of money, Bhai and other top leaders . . . travelled around explaining that Congress could not give the voter any of the facilities . . . offered by the opposition. . . . 'I ask you,' he said, 'to treat this day of polling as a pilgrimage. . . . '

Polling Day . . . was a day not to be easily forgotten. . . . The villagers came out in thousands on foot, on cycles and in bullock carts. . . . All were dressed in their holiday best . . . with the Congress flag bravely fluttering in the breeze.

The opposition parties had made a big effort to seduce the voter, and there were extra buses plying the roads. . . . At intervals there were arrangements for snacks – iced *sherbets* . . . and other things the village people eat on days of rejoicing. But the buses remained empty and nobody went to the places where the tempting food was available. Straight to the polling booths they went, singing, joking, happy. And the most moving sight of all was that, having cast their vote, they opened their meagre little bundles of parched rice or grain and ate under the shade of the trees. . . . It came to a point where the agents of the opposition, seeing all the good food being wasted in such large quantities, begged our voters to go and have some even if they voted Congress. . . . The invitations were refused. . . . I thought to myself, 'These are the people of India. They and they alone will give the final answer. . . . How right Bapu is – we must never forget them. . . . ' But alas for . . . India, we keep forgetting them. . . . In every crisis in India the faceless multitude has rallied to uphold the great ideals on which our civilization has been based, but what have *we* done, the so-called leaders, the educated, the 'upper' classes?

Congress won a striking victory in eight out of the eleven British provinces, and the leaders of Congress parties were invited by the governors to form ministries. . . . The provinces were under the direct rule of the Viceroy, whereas a vast territory, about two-fifths of the whole of India, was under the rule of Princes who had accepted paramountcy of the British crown. . . .

V. L. Pandit, *The Scope of Happiness*, Weidenfeld & Nicolson, 1979, pp. 125–7, 129–31

Questions

a What was 'Congress' (line 16), and who were 'Bhai' (line 26) and 'Bapu' (line 48)?

b Why did the Government of India Act, 1935, not satisfy the Congress Party?

c What disadvantages did Mrs Pandit and her husband, Ranjit, face in the elections? How did Congress supporters compensate for these on polling day?

d What features of this account help to explain the eventual self-government of India in 1947?

* e To what specific crisis in India in recent years is the author's comment (lines 48−51) relevant?

* f What problems do autobiographies pose for the historian?

* g Explain the growth of Indian nationalism in the twentieth century.

3 1947

By the time Lord Wavell left India, the general situation was so bleak that it looked as though the country was heading for certain disaster. . . . The precarious food position, the steadily deteriorating economic situation, and widespread labour unrest added to the threatening symptoms of a
5 general collapse. . . .

Lord Mountbatten arrived in Delhi on 22 March 1947. . . . Even before he was sworn in, [he] wrote to Gandhiji and Jinnah inviting them to Delhi for discussion. . . .

He said . . . that His Majesty's Government were resolved to transfer
10 power by June 1948 . . . [which] meant that a solution had to be reached within the next few months . . . he appealed to everyone to do his best to avoid any word or action which might lead to further communal bitterness or add to the toll of innocent victims . . .

Lord Mountbatten had a remarkably careful yet quick and businesslike
15 method of working. As soon as he finished an interview with a leader, and before proceeding to the next, he would dictate a résumé of the talk, a copy of which would be circulated to each member of his staff. He held staff conferences every day, sometimes twice and even thrice a day, to study and discuss how events were shaping. . . .
20 Consultation with the Governors certainly gave [him] a good idea of the colossal administrative difficulties involved in a transfer of power based on partition. But the problem that actually confronted him was, if it became inevitable to divide the country—and Lord Mountbatten was sure that no other solution would be acceptable to Jinnah − how was this to
25 be brought about with the willing concurrence of the parties concerned? The greater the insistence by Jinnah on his province-wide Pakistan, the stronger was the Congress demand that he should not be allowed to carry unwilling minorities with him. Nehru . . . declared: 'The Muslim League can have Pakistan . . . but on the condition that they do not take
30 away other parts of India which do not wish to join Pakistan.' . . .

Within six weeks of his arrival . . . Lord Mountbatten had produced a plan which marked the first stage towards the transfer of power. In all his discussions with party leaders and others, despite the divergent views which he was forced to adjust and reconcile, there was nowhere any
35 evidence of an attempt to question either his own impartiality or the bona fides of His Majesty's Government. . . .

It would have been an ideal arrangement if [he] could have stayed on as Governor-General of both the Dominions. But even as Governor-General of India, he could still be of immense service. . . . It was his
40 personality . . . that had helped to bring about some measure of common action . . . and had prevented a bad situation from getting worse. . . . [His] presence would be of great help in solving the problem of the Indian States. It would also have a reassuring effect on serving British officers, particularly in the Armed Forces, where their retention for at least some
45 time was indispensable. . . .

The communal holocaust, the two-way exodus of refugees . . . all these provided the Government of India . . . with a task which was as stupendous as any nation ever had to face. If in its initial stages the situation had not been controlled with determination and vigour, the
50 consequences would have brought down the Government itself. It is to the eternal credit of Lord Mountbatten that he agreed to take over the helm of responsibility at that critical stage, and it redounds to the statesmanship of Nehru and Patel that they unhesitatingly and confidently offered it to him. . . . .

55 The main factor responsible for the early transfer of power was the return of the Labour Party . . . in 1945 . . . .

The British Government's decision to quit India not only touched the hearts and stirred the emotions of Indians; it produced an immediate reassuring effect on the whole of South-East Asia and earned for
60 Britain . . . universal respect and goodwill. . . .

V. P. Menon [Constitutional Adviser to the Governor-General, 1942–7], *The Transfer of Power in India*, Longman, 1957, pp. 348, 350–52, 354, 357, 394–5, 434, 436–7

Questions

a   What were the two political parties in India, and who led them?
b   Which government was in power in Britain in 1947? Why did it favour independence for India?
c   Examine Lord Mountbatten's contribution to the problems of India in 1947. Why do you think he was chosen to be the last Viceroy?
d   Is the author too optimistic about the events he is describing?
* e   What had been the importance to Britain of India during the Second World War?
* f   'The Communal holocaust, the two-way exodus of refugees . . .' (line 46). Investigate these problems and their effect on the new states.

4 From Viceroy to Governor-General

It is barely six months ago that Mr Attlee invited me to accept the appointment of last Viceroy. He made it clear that this would be no easy task – since His Majesty's Government . . . had decided to transfer power to Indian hands by June 1948. At that time it seemed to many that 5 [the] . . . Government had set a date far too early. How could this tremendous operation be completed in 15 months?

However, I had not been more than a week in India before I realised that this date . . . was too late rather than too early; communal tension and rioting had assumed proportions of which I had had no conception 10 when I left England. It seemed to me that a decision had to be taken at the earliest possible moment unless there was to be risk of a general conflagration throughout the whole sub-continent.

I entered into discussions with the leaders of all the parties at once – and the result was the plan of June 3rd. Its acceptance has been hailed as an 15 example of fine statesmanship throughout the world. The plan was evolved at every stage by a process of open diplomacy with the leaders. Its success is chiefly attributable to them. . . .

At the very meeting at which the plan of June 3rd was accepted . . . we set up machinery which was to carry out one of the 20 greatest administrative operations in history – the partition of a sub-continent of 400 million inhabitants and the transfer of power to two independent governments in less than two and a half months. . . .

I know well that the rejoicing which the advent of freedom brings is tempered . . . by the sadness that it could not come to a united India; and 25 that the pain of division has shorn today's events of some of its joy. In supporting your leaders in the difficult decision which they had to take, you have displayed as much magnanimity and realism as have those patriotic statesmen themselves. . . .

The tasks before you are heavy. The war ended two years ago. In fact it 30 was on this very day two years ago that I was with that great friend of India, Mr Attlee in his Cabinet Room when the news came through that Japan had surrendered. That was a moment for thankfulness and rejoicing, for it marked the end of six bitter years of destruction and slaughter. But in India we have achieved something greater – what has 35 been well described as 'A treaty of Peace without a War.' India, which played such a valiant part, as I can personally testify from my experience in South-East Asia, has also had to pay her price in the dislocation of her economy and the casualties to her gallant fighting men. . . . Preoccupations with the political problem retarded recovery. 40 It is for you to ensure the happiness and ever-increasing prosperity of the people, to provide against future scarcities of food, cloth and essential commodities and to build up a balanced economy. . . .

At this historic moment, let us not forget all that India owes to Mahatma Gandhi – the architect of her freedom through non-45 violence. . . .

In your first Prime Minister, Pandit Jawaharlal Nehru, you have a

world-renowned leader of courage and vision. His trust and friendship
have helped me beyond measure in my task. Under his able guidance,
assisted by the colleagues whom he has selected . . . India will now attain
50 a position of strength and influence and take her rightful place in the
comity of nations.

> Viscount Mountbatten of Burma, Address to the India Con-
> stituent Assembly at New Delhi, 15 August 1947, in *Speeches by*
> *His Excellency Rear-Admiral The Earl Mountbatten of Burma*, 1949,
> pp. 30–31, 33

Questions

a Why did Mountbatten advance the date for self-government?
b What problems did this cause?
c What examples are there here of Mountbatten's statesmanship and
   suitability for the posts he held in India?
* *d* 'Divide and rule, then divide and quit.' Is this a valid comment on
   Britain in India?
* *e* Examine the role of Gandhi and Nehru in the struggle for Indian
   independence.
* *f* Was partition desirable in view of the fact that neither on geographical
   nor on religious grounds was it possible to divide the sub-continent?

5 Nationalisation of the Canal

This, O citizens, is the battle into which we are now plunged. This . . . is
the battle in which we are now involved. It is a battle against imperialism
and the methods and tactics of imperialism, and a battle against Israel, the
vanguard of imperialism, which was created by imperialism in an effort
5 to annihilate our nationalism in the same way as it annihilated
Palestine. . . .

Britain left Egypt, believing . . . that she could have no place there.
This was because the people of Egypt were awakened; because [they] had
pledged themselves to achieve for Egypt freedom of life. . . . As I told
10 you, Arab nationalism has been set on fire from the Atlantic Ocean to the
Persian Gulf. Arab nationalism feels its existence, its structure and
strength. It also believes in its right to life. These are the battles which we
are entering.

We can never say that the battle of Algeria is not our battle. Nor can we
15 say that Jordan's December battle was not our battle. . . .

The Suez Canal was dug by the efforts of the sons of Egypt – 120,000
Egyptians died in the process. The Suez Canal Company, sitting in Paris,
is a usurping company. It usurped our concessions. When he came here de
Lesseps acted in the same manner as do certain people who come to hold
20 talks with me. Does history repeat itself? On the contrary! We shall build
the High Dam . . . as we desire. . . . The Canal company annually takes
£35,000,000. Why shouldn't we take it ourselves? . . .

The Suez Canal was one of the façades of oppression, extortion, and humiliation. Today . . . the Suez Canal has been nationalized and this decree has . . . been published . . . and made law. Today . . . we declare that our property has been returned to us. . . .

At this moment . . . some of your Egyptian brethren are proceeding to administer the canal company and to run its affairs . . . and to control shipping in the canal. . . .

> Speech by Colonel Nasser, 26 July 1956, in D. C. Watt (ed.), *Documents on the Suez Crisis, 26 July to 6 November 1956*, 1957, pp. 44-5, 48-9

Questions

a When and why was the Suez Canal dug? Who owned it, and what was its importance to the West?

b What was the 'High Dam' (line 21)? What advantage would it give to Egypt, and why was there a problem over the finance for it?

* c What were 'the battle of Algeria' (line 14) and 'Jordan's December battle' (line 15)?

* d What comments were made in the West about Nasser's claim that Egyptians had begun 'to control shipping in the canal' (lines 28 – 9)?

* e Examine the background to Arab-Israeli problems, in the light of Nasser's comment on Israel being 'created by imperialism . . . to annihilate our nationalism . . . as it annihilated Palestine' (lines 4 – 6). Why did Nasser seize the Canal in 1956?

* f Outline the reaction of the West to the nationalisation of the Canal.

6 The Ultimatum

The Governments of the United Kingdom and France have taken note of the outbreak of hostilities between Israel and Egypt. This event threatens to disrupt the freedom of navigation through the Suez Canal on which the economic life of many nations depends.

The Governments of the United Kingdom and France are resolved to do all in their power to bring about the early cessation of hostilities and to safeguard the free passage of the Canal.

They accordingly request the Government of Israel:

(a) to stop all warlike action on land, sea and air forthwith;

(b) to withdraw all Israeli military forces to a distance of 10 miles east of the Canal.

A communication has been addressed to the Government of Egypt, requesting them to cease hostilities and to withdraw their forces from the neighbourhood of the Canal, and to accept the temporary occupation by Anglo-French forces of key positions at Port Said, Ismailia and Suez.

The United Kingdom and French Governments request an answer to this communication within 12 hours. If at the expiration of that time one or both Governments have not undertaken to comply with the above

requirements, United Kingdom and French forces will intervene in
20 whatever strength may be necessary to secure compliance.

> Anglo-French Ultimatum to the Governments of Egypt and
> Israel, 30 October 1956 [text as laid in the Library of the House of
> Commons], in D. C. Watt (ed.) *Documents on the Suez Crisis, 26
> July to 6 November 1956*, 1957, pp. 85−6

Questions

a Why were Britain and France interested in this dispute?
b Why was the request to Israel and Egypt (lines 8−15) unfair to Egypt?
c Why should Anglo-French forces occupy the chosen positions (lines
   14−15)?
* d Was any reason offered by Britain or France as to why neither the
   United Nations nor the United States was consulted?
* e Study the military aspects of the war, and then comment on the
   positions and strength of Israeli forces on 30 October.

7 Collusion?

Challe [Deputy Chief of Staff for the French Air Force] then proceeded
to outline what he termed a possible plan of action for Britain and France
to gain physical control of the Suez Canal. The plan . . . was that Israel
should be invited to attack Egypt across the Sinai Peninsula and that
5 France and Britain, having given the Israeli forces enough time to seize all
or most of Sinai, should then order 'both sides' to withdraw their forces
from the Suez Canal, in order to permit an Anglo-French force to
intervene and occupy the Canal on the pretext of saving it from damage
by fighting. Thus the two powers would be able to claim to be 'separating
10 the combatants' and 'extinguishing a dangerous fire', while actually
seizing control of the entire waterway and of its terminal ports, Port
Said and Suez. This would not only restore the running of the Canal to
Anglo-French management, but, by putting us physically in control
of the terminal ports . . . it would enable us to supervise all shipping
15 movements through the Canal and so to break the Egyptian blockade of
Israel.

    Nothing was said at this stage about the timing of these operations,
although it was made fairly clear to us that the French wanted as little
delay as possible. Likewise, the military plan was not discussed in any
20 detail, Challe merely suggesting that a combined sea-borne and para-
troop invasion should suffice. . . . It was clear that the French had made
at least preliminary soundings with the Israeli Government. . . .

    Doing his best to conceal his excitement, Eden replied non-committ-
ally that he would give these suggestions very careful thought. . . .
25   I knew . . . that no matter what contrary advice he might receive over
the next forty-eight hours, the Prime Minister had already made up his
mind to go along with the French plan . . . and we were to ally ourselves

with the Israelis and the French in an attack on Egypt designed to topple
Nasser and to seize the Suez Canal. . . .

30 The decks were being cleared for action, and it was plain that,
whatever consultations I might hold with the Foreign Office advisers and
however strongly they might support me in warning against this venture,
the Prime Minister was not going to be gainsaid. Nothing was now to be
done which might upset Israel or divert her attention from the main
target, Nasser's Egypt. . . .

35 Instead of negotiating our way back to a position of control over the
[Canal] . . ., we were to occupy the Canal and the terminal ports. One
act of seizure was to be followed by another and . . . relations would be
poisoned between Britain and Egypt and the Arab world for generations
to come. To make matters even worse, Britain had obviously used Israel
40 as her stalking-horse for this exercise. For if proof were needed of
collusion between Britain and the aggressor, it was written plainly
enough in the timing of the ultimatum, which demanded that both
belligerents withdraw to a distance of ten miles from the Canal at a
moment when the Egyptian army was still engaging the Israelis at
45 distances between 75 and 125 miles to the east of the Canal. This meant
that, at the moment of its issue, the powers who were pretending to put a
stop to the fighting by separating the belligerents were ordering one of
them – and the victim of aggression at that – to withdraw up to 135
miles, while the other, who happened to be the aggressor, was told to
50 advance on all fronts between 65 and 115 miles! . . .

[In the Commons on 31 October the Foreign Secretary, Selwyn
Lloyd, was asked about collusion. He replied:] 'The Right Hon.
Gentleman asked whether there had been collusion with regard to this
matter. Every time any incident has happened on the frontiers of Israel
55 and the Arab states we have been accused of being in collusion with the
Israelis about it. That allegation has been broadcast from Radio Cairo
every time. It is quite wrong to state that Israel was incited to this action
by Her Majesty's Government. There was no prior agreement between
us about it. It is, of course, true that the Israeli mobilisation gave some
60 advance warning and we urged restraint upon the Israeli Government
and in particular drew attention to the serious consequences of any attack
upon Jordan.'

A. Nutting, *No End of a Lesson*, Constable, 1967, pp. 93 – 5, 116,
126

Questions

a Challe put forward his plan of action at Chequers on 14 October.
What was it, and how did it accord with the Anglo-French
ultimatum (document 6)?

b How was this plan to be explained to the world at large?

c What was Eden's reaction to the French suggestions? Where did
Nutting suggest that he might meet opposition?

d In Selwyn Lloyd's speech, what importance should be attached to

Israel being 'incited to this action by Her Majesty's Government'
(lines 57–8) and 'there was no prior agreement between us . . .' (lines
58–9)?

* *e* In December 1956, Eden claimed in the Commons that 'there was not
foreknowledge that Israel would attack Egypt.' Was this true? What
was always at the back of Eden's mind during this crisis?

* *f* If in fact there was collusion at Sèvres on 23 October between Britain,
France and Israel, is this significant in the context of earlier secret
agreements in the twentieth century, for example, the Treaty of
London, 1915, or the Sykes-Picot agreement, 1916?

Further Work

a In 1917, Britain had declared in favour of 'the gradual development
of self-governing institutions with a view to the progressive
realization of responsible government as an integral part of the British
Empire.' What progress had been made on this by 1939?

b 'Partition is a spiritual tragedy. I do not agree with what my closest
friends are doing; thirty-two years of work have come to an
inglorious end.' (Gandhi) Discuss the wisdom of partition in 1947.

c Viceroy of India was only one of Earl Mountbatten of Burma's high
positions. In what other ways was his long career a memorable one?

d 'Perhaps the most damaging of all factors which prevented the British
and French actions from winning any degree of international support
was the immediate acceptance by considerable sections of opinion of
allegations that the British and French governments either had
definite foreknowledge of the Israeli attack on Egypt, or that their
ultimatum and intervention were concerted with the Israeli
government.' (D. C. Watt)
   Discuss this statement on the failure of the Anglo-French
intervention, especially with regard to UN and US opinion.

e Why is it so difficult for historians to establish the exact details of what
happened in 1956?

f Earl Mountbatten, First Sea Lord in 1956, said afterwards, 'I think
he [Eden] wasn't very well.' Have historians neglected the
psychological and medical state of historical figures (cf. the quotation
from R. R. James on p. 5)?

g Examine the significance of the Suez Crisis to Britain and the world.
What was its connection with the Soviet invasion of Hungary in
1956, and with the relations between Britain and the United States?

X An Indian Summer – the Conservatives in Power 1951–64

Introduction

Views of the period of Conservative governments from 1951 to 1964 vacillate between the critique espoused by the Left, of 'Thirteen Wasted Years', the view expressed by some economists of an 'affluent society' and the view of many historians of this as a period of 'illusion'. Was this period one of Indian summer, an 'Edwardian' era which preceded a period of crisis? Could Macmillan have said '*Après moi, le déluge*'?

The Conservatives came to power in the 1951 General Election largely because the electorate were disillusioned by Labour. The exigencies of 'Austerity' were remembered more clearly than the benefits of the 'Welfare State'. The removal of the symbols of austerity, especially rationing, the housing programme masterminded by Harold Macmillan and the boom of the early fifties all presaged well for the Conservatives. They were aided in this by the internecine struggles within the Labour Party between Gaitskell and Bevan over the succession.

This chapter aims to consider how well the Conservatives did in dealing with the economic problems facing them at home. It is important, however, not to view this question in isolation. You should make reference to Conservative attitudes to Egypt and to the end of Empire since, it has been argued, they too reflect the unreality of government policy.

Galbraith's book on the affluent society published in 1958 was seen by many as symbolising attitudes in the late fifties. Though primarily concerned with the United States, his work was hailed in Britain as a masterpiece which truly reflected the nature of her society. His work fitted the mood of the British at the time. Austerity with its characteristic lack of consumer goods was replaced by affluence with the plethora of consumer products which still characterise the country. However, not everyone fell under the Galbraith spell. M. Shanks' work on the stagnant society, published in 1961, showed another side to the economy and government policy. He saw Conservative policy as leading to inflation based on consumer demand, and thought that there was a failure to deal adequately with the problems facing the economy.

P. Calvocoressi provides a longer perspective on the British economy. He sees the failure of successive governments to deal with it as the result of their unwillingness to dismantle the 'mixed' economy of private and public sectors. This view, though not his critique of western democratic capitalism, certainly accords with that put forward by V. Bogdanor and R. Skidelsky. They see 'consensus' as the basis of government policy between 1951 and 1964. The uncritical acceptance by both major political parties of this concept meant that new perspectives for examining old problems could not be forthcoming. The illusion of continued affluence, as well as the idea of maintaining a world role, were the result of this. Finally, A. Sked and C. Cook look at the question from a slightly broader viewpoint. Politics may have remained the same but, they argue, society did not. New values, new beliefs and new attitudes began to show themselves. In this way the idea of consensus came into question, and the illusion of affluence was made clear.

Further Reading

In addition to the general works by C. J. Bartlett, P. Calvocoressi, L. J. Macfarlane, L. A. Monk and A. Sked and C. Cook cited in chapter VIII, the following are valuable:

V. Bogdanor and R. Skidelsky (eds), *The Age of Affluence 1951−1964* (Macmillan, 1970)

D. McKie and C. Cook (eds), *The Decade of Disillusion: British Politics in the 1960's* (Macmillan, 1972)

M. Proudfoot, *British Politics and Government 1951−1970: a study of an Affluent Society* (Faber, 1974), a straightforward account of this period laid out thematically.

On the economic policies of this period see:

A. Budd, *The Politics of Economic Planning* (Fontana, 1978), the simplest starting point on a complex subject.

* J. C. R. Dow, *The Management of the British Economy 1945−60* (Cambridge, 1964)

* S. Brittan, *Steering the Economy* (1971) a more detailed account of Treasury attitudes.

Autobiographical or biographical material is rather thin on the ground:

H. Pelling, *Winston Churchill* (Macmillan, 1974)

F. Williams, *A Prime Minister Remembers* (Heinemann, 1961)

R. A. Butler, *The Art of the Possible* (Hamish Hamilton, 1971)

H. Macmillan, *Memoirs 1914−1963* (6 vols, Macmillan 1966−73), they often tell the historian more about the man than about the times. A critical biography of Macmillan is needed.

On the Conservative party itself during this period:

J. Barnes, *From Affluence to Disillusion 1940−1974* (Longman, forthcoming)

R. Blake, *The Conservative Party from Peel to Churchill* (Fontana, 1976)

For the flavour of the times there is little to better watching John Osborne's play *Look Back in Anger* or listening to some early rock music. They reflect ordinary preoccupations much better than do economic policy and theorising.

1   The Illusion

As with individuals so with nations. And the experience of nations with well-being is exceedingly brief. Nearly all, throughout history, have been very poor. The exception, almost insignificant in the whole span of human existence, has been the last few generations in the comparatively small corner of the world populated by Europeans. Here, and especially in the United States, there has been great and quite unprecedented affluence.

The ideas by which the people of this favoured part of the world interpret their existence, and in measure guide their behaviour, were not forged in the world of wealth. These ideas were the product of a world in which poverty had been man's normal lot, and any other state was in degree unimaginable. This poverty was not the elegant torture of the spirit which comes from contemplating another man's more spacious possessions. It was the unedifying mortification of the flesh – from hunger, sickness and cold. Those who might be freed temporarily from such burden could not know when it would strike again, for at best hunger yielded only perilously to privation. It is improbable that the poverty of the masses of the people was made greatly more bearable by the fact that a very few – those upon whose movements nearly all recorded history centres – were very rich.

No one would wish to argue that the ideas which interpret this world of grim scarcity would serve well for the contemporary United States. Poverty was the all-pervasive fact of that world. Obviously it is not of ours. One would not expect that the preoccupations of a poverty-ridden world would be relevant in one where the ordinary individual has access to amenities – foods, entertainment, personal transportation and plumbing – in which not even the rich rejoiced a century ago. So great has been the change that many of the desires of the individual are no longer evident to him. They become so only as they are synthesised, elaborated, and nurtured by advertising and salesmanship, and these, in turn, have become among our most important and talented professions. Few people at the beginning of the nineteenth century needed an ad-man to tell him what he wanted.

It would be wrong to suggest that the economic ideas which once interpreted the world of mass poverty have made no adjustment to the world of affluence. There have been many adjustments, including some which have gone unrecognised or have been poorly understood. But there has also been a remarkable resistance. And the total alteration in underlying circumstances has not been squarely faced. As a result we are guided, in part, by ideas that are relevant to another world; and as a further result we do many things that are unnecessary, some that are unwise, and a few that are insane. We enhance substantially the risk of depression and thereby the threat to our affluence itself. . . .

No student of social matters in these days can escape feeling how precarious is the existence of that with which he deals. Western man has escaped for the moment the poverty which was for long his all-

embracing fate. . . . The affluent country which conducts its affairs in accordance with rules of another and poorer age also forgoes opportunities. And in misunderstanding itself it will, in any time of
50 difficulty, implacably prescribe for itself the wrong remedies. . . .

J. K. Galbraith, *The Affluent Society*, 1958, Penguin edn 1969, pp. 31—2, 34

Questions

a (i) What does 'affluence' (line 7) mean?
(ii) In what way has 'poverty . . . been man's normal lot' (line 11)?
(iii) What does Galbraith mean when he talks of the rich being those on whom 'nearly all recorded history centres' (lines 19—20)?
(iv) What are 'amenities' (line 26)?
(v) What is an 'ad-man' (line 32)?
* *b* Who is J. K. Galbraith and why is he an important source for attitudes during the 1950s and early 1960s?
c Galbraith sees the world in terms of affluence and poverty. Is this a valid perspective?
d How far does Galbraith's view of society accord with that of Britain in the 1950s?
e Galbraith may have believed in affluence but he certainly saw its dangers. Discuss.
* *f* What enabled the western world to pull ahead of the rest of the world? When did this occur?

2   The Reality?

For economic growth is no longer restrained in the West by technical ignorance, as it was in many ways until the 1940's. There is no lack of new ideas, of new techniques or machines; nor is there any serious lack of knowledge of how the economic system works. We are no longer
5   powerless to avert depressions or to prevent massive unemployment. We are no longer compelled to look on powerless at the catastrophic fluctuations of the trade cycle, unpredictable as a force of nature. If we cannot tame this monster now, it is due to incompetence and not ignorance. . . .
10   And yet it works much less smoothly. Why is this? Three main reasons stand out, all interconnected. The first is that the measures required to contain inflation, unlike those required to stimulate demand, are unpleasant and painful. It is much easier psychologically and politically to encourage people to do things they would like to do but are afraid
15   to . . . than to stop them doing what they would normally want to do. . . . So in taking action to curb excessive demand, a Government is acting contrary to the natural desires of its people and is therefore bound to encounter all sorts of frictions – especially in a democracy. . . .
The second reason is rather more complicated. Inflation manifests itself

20 in a tendency for production costs and prices to rise sharply and
progressively. That is why, in a perfectly competitive world with
international free trade, inflations and depressions should both be self-
correcting – through the operation of the price mechanism. . . . In the
real world things don't happen quite like that, but it is true that a country
25 like Britain which depends on international trade cannot let its costs and
prices get out of line with the rest of the world because of the danger to its
balance of payments. . . . However, while the basic cause of inflation is
excessive demand, the rise in costs can itself be an autonomous and partly
self-generating inflationary element. For example, it is possible to
30 'import' inflation – and indeed this was largely what happened in Britain
in the early post-war years. Because of the swing in the terms of trade in
those years the cost of our imports rose sharply. This had two effects.
Industries were faced with mounting raw material costs, while they
naturally tried to pass this on to the consumer in higher prices. Wage-
35 earners, faced with a higher cost of living, sought to reimburse themselves
by pay increases. . . . In this way the familiar inflationary spiral of rising
wages and rising prices got under way. . . .

The third reason for the difficulty of imposing an effective anti-
inflationary policy is that one is making a real choice between evils. The
40 object of every economic system is to increase the supply and the range of
consumer goods and services available to its people – in other words, to
increase the standard of living as fast as possible. In the long run, this can
only be done by expanding production. It goes against the
grain . . . deliberately to reverse this process and slow down the rate of
45 expansion; and Governments are understandably reluctant to do so.
What makes things worse is that . . . the sector of production which is
most responsive to Government action is capital investment. . . . To cut
back investment in order to maintain and increase consumption is to
mortgage the future for the present. But this is what in fact happens when
50 the Government tries to limit demand. . . . In 1951 at the top of the
Korean boom Mr Hugh Gaitskell . . . introduced a Budget which was
deliberately designed to 'soak up' excess purchasing power by allowing
prices to rise. One result of this policy was to sweep away completely the
rather shaky edifice of wage restraint built up under his predecessor Sir
55 Stafford Cripps, and to bring about a massive round of wage claims. In
1955, when, as a result of a Government-assisted boom in industrial
investment, demand began to run ahead of capacity and the economy
became overstrained, . . . Mr R. A. Butler adopted roughly the same
expedient. The cost of living was deliberately pushed up by raising
60 purchase tax on a wide range of goods, and at the same time a number of
measures were taken to discourage capital investment. Mr Butler's policy
was followed by his two successors at the Treasury. . . . It was only
reversed at the onset of the recession in 1958.

What did this policy achieve? It did eventually succeed in slowing
65 down the pace of wage increases, which was one of the main factors
behind the 1955 inflation. But it took nearly three years to do so, at the
cost of a virtually complete industrial standstill and a number of financial

crises and major industrial disputes. . . . One particularly unfortunate
aspect of this period was the Government's attempts to restrict invest-
70 ment in the public sector – an attempt which was largely unsuccessful
because of the long-term nature of most of the projects involved, which
made it quite impossible to turn them on and off like a tap to meet the
short-term fluctuations in the economy.

It is too early to assess the long-term damage to the British economy
75 from this period of enforced standstill, but it certainly left us with a lot of
leeway to catch up. . . .

M. Shanks, *The Stagnant Society*, 1961, Penguin edn 1971, pp. 30,
33–9, 40–42

Questions

a (i) In the passage Shanks uses a number of economic terms. What do
the following mean: 'economic growth' (line 1), 'the trade cycle' (line
7), 'inflation' (line 12), 'balance of payments' (line 27), 'capital
investment' (line 47), and 'the public sector' (line 70)?
(ii) Who were Mr Hugh Gaitskell (line 51), Sir Stafford Cripps (line
55) and Mr R. A. Butler (line 58)?
(iii) What was 'the Korean boom' (lines 50–1)?
(iv) Who were Mr Butler's two successors at the Treasury' (line 62)?

b What were the three main reasons why the economy did not function
as smoothly as it should have done in the early fifties, according to
Shanks?

c How did the government attempt to resolve the short-term fluctuations in the economy and with what results?

d Shanks calls the period from 1950 to 1958 'the years the locusts ate'.
How accurate a description is this of the economy?

e The early to mid-1950s saw the British economy going through a
period of crisis. Government action did little to resolve the problem.
Discuss.

* *f* Given the economic condition of Britain in 1958 and the forecasts
being made for its development, it is difficult to talk of affluence.
Comment.

3   The Crunch

Two parties shared between them the government of Britain in the thirty
years that followed the second world war. Both had as a prime aim the
restoration and expansion of the British economy by restoring and
expanding industry and exports. Both failed. The economic decline of
5 Britain they inherited accelerated.

In Britain the conduct of public affairs is accompanied by intelligent
and sophisticated comment and debate. In this debate the focus
throughout these years was on what the government of the day was
doing, on whether it was doing the right things or the wrong. The
10 formulation is significant. It shows how government action and

government policy had become central. The role of government in the direction and management of the economy had become paramount, even though many . . . deplored or sought to evade this development.

Every government acted within the established system. None tried
15 radically to change it. This system was and remained a capitalist system. Labour governments made significant changes in emphasis with the system by acts of nationalization which diminished the area of private capitalism and extended the public sector, but there had long been these two sectors and both were and remained capitalist in structure and
20 operation. The mixed economy . . . was mixed in different proportions. . . .

What then were governments trying to do? There was not so much difference between them . . . and [the differences] were ineffective. All governments accepted an obligation to contribute positively to the
25 prosperity of both sectors. This contribution was in the nature of things financial; governments provided money or facilitated credit, and with this money private and nationalized businesses would invest, modernise and grow. At the same time . . . governments of both colours also saw it as part of their job to intervene in economic affairs to keep wages in
30 check, whether by bargaining with the unions or by subsidizing the cost of living by law. . . . Government intervention of this nature was inflationary. . . . A modern democratic capitalist economy is based on inflation, and in these years the wherewithal for recovery and expansion was provided to a significant degree by government. . . .
35 Whatever their causes, failures led to political division and criticism not only of the policies of government but also its role. Governments had disagreed over the right means to stimulate the mixed capitalist economy, but they had not denied that this was something that governments ought to be doing. Still less had they questioned the existence of the mixed
40 economy. But the failures of this economy . . . led to questions about the viability of such an economy.

P. Calvocoressi *The British Experience 1945−75*, Penguin, 1978,
pp. 105−12

Questions

a (i) In what ways did 'the economic decline of Britain they inherited' 'acclerate'? (lines 4−5)

(ii) In what ways did 'The role of government . . . become paramount' (lines 11−12)?

(iii) What are 'the capitalist system' (line 15) and 'acts of nationalization' (line 17)?

(iv) In what ways were 'The mixed economy . . . mixed in different proportions' (lines 20−21)?

(v) How did government subsidise 'the cost of living by law' (lines 30−31)?

* b Calvocoressi takes a longer perspective of Britain than the other

authors in this chapter. How valuable is his view in examining the
thirteen years of Conservative rule from 1951 to 1964?

c The failure of government between 1951 and 1964 to deliver the
   goods had important economic and political results. Discuss.

d The Conservative governments of the 1950s and early 1960s were ill-
   suited to deal with the economic problems facing them. How true is
   this statement?

* e It was capitalism not government that failed in the 1950s. Comment.

4 The Thirteen Years – a View

Ten years ago it was possible, and indeed usual, to look back to the 1950's
as an age of prosperity and achievement. This was certainly the verdict of
the electorate which in 1959 returned a Conservative Government to
power with a handsome majority, for the third time running. Today we
5 are more likely to remember the whole period as an age of illusion, of
missed opportunities, with Macmillan as the magician whose wonderful
act kept us too long distracted from reality. . . . what has altered the
verdict on the 1950's has been the experience of the troubles of the 1960's,
which stem in part at least from the neglect of the earlier decade. Already
10 by 1964 the appeal of the slogan 'Thirteen Wasted Years' was strong
enough to give Labour a tiny majority; in the years following it has been
confirmed almost as the conventional wisdom . . . . Perhaps the period
of Conservative rule will be looked upon as the last period of quiet before
the storm, rather like the Edwardian age which in many respects it
15 resembles. In that case its tranquillity will come to be valued more highly
than its omissions.

The illusion with the most profound consequences was the economic
one. In his book *The Affluent Society* (1958), J. K. Galbraith intended to
sketch an outline of a developed society which had in large part solved the
20 problem of production, and could concentrate its energies on other
things. The class struggle was obsolete; so also were the ideologies which
sought to justify it. Politics would no longer involve large general choices
but disagreement over more limited and piecemeal issues.

Uncritical transference of Galbraith's thesis into the British context
25 helped obscure the fact that Britain had not, in fact, solved its economic
problems. The optimism of the early 1950's is, however, perfectly
understandable. . . . But this miracle was built on temporary and
fortuitous circumstances. From 1955, Britain was bedevilled by a series of
sterling crises which gradually forced upon the attention of politicians
30 problems they wished to avoid.

It is now possible to see that for Britain the years 1951 – 64 were neither
a period of continuous and uninterrupted expansion as the Conservatives
would have us believe, nor the 'Thirteen Wasted Years' of Labour
mythology. . . .

35 In 1962 Dean Acheson said, 'Britain has lost an empire; she has not yet
found a role'. . . . the failure to rethink her world role was as evident in

diplomacy as in economics. Macmillan foresaw and expedited the final liquidation of Empire, but he had few ideas about what to put in its place. . . . The special relationship with the United States was to remain
40 the cornerstone of British policy. But without the Empire, this relationship was bound to become increasingly one between master and servant. . . . These illusions blinded Macmillan . . . to the far-reaching changes occurring in Europe. . . . The rhetoric of the world role remained essential to the Conservatives, who still saw themselves as an
45 imperial party; essential also to the Labour Party, whose moral ambitions remained world-wide. . . .

What is the explanation for these illusions? For we are of course dealing not with one illusion but with several, which reacted upon, and reinforced, each other. . . . At the political level these psychological
50 factors revealed themselves in consensus. In economics, as in foreign policy, consensus reigned. Consensus is, indeed, a fundamental idea in understanding the politics of the 1950's. It signified acceptance of the mixed economy and the Welfare State. From this point of view, it did entail a real humanising and civilising of the political
55 battle. . . . Consensus did ensure the emancipation of politics from the ghosts of the past; unfortunately it also imposed a moratorium on the raising of new and vital issues. For consensus also signified acceptance of traditional assumptions concerning Britain's political and economic role in the world. Thus real and important political choices came to be
60 submerged in a generalised commitment to the objective of economic growth.

Economic growth was essential to the consensus. It enabled the Conservatives to offer for the first time a viable alternative to Socialism with their idea of property-owning democracy. No one need be defeated
65 in the class war because no war was being fought. Capitalism could provide affluence for the working class while at the same time preserving the gains of the well-to-do. . . . Consensus was the natural product of a lessening class antagonism, which in turn reflected a seeming trend towards embourgeoisement. . . . Indeed, one of the striking charac-
70 teristics of the 1950's was the absence of any major intellectual challenge to the dominant political assumptions. . . .

The politics to which consensus gave rise was one which reacted to events, but it was not able to provide the imaginative understanding needed to confront the future. For this the inherited framework was
75 inadequate. . . . For during the 1950's it was gradually discovered that the questions vital to Britain's future could not be discussed within the confines of the party system and the political conventions which surrounded it.

V. Bogdanor and R. Skidelsky *The Age of Affluence 1951–64*, Macmillan, 1970, pp. 7–11, 15

Questions

a Why have attitudes to the 1951–64 period changed?

*   *b* How far does this change reflect the fact that people rewrite history in terms of their own experiences?
    c What were the main illusions which the authors identify in the passage? Why did contemporaries believe that these were realities?
    d In what ways is the idea of 'consensus' the key to understanding attitudes in the fifties and early sixties?
*   *e* Assess the role of Harold Macmillan as 'the magician whose wonderful act kept us too long distracted from reality' (lines 6–7).
*   *f* In what ways was the period of Conservative rule from 1951 to 1964 an 'Edwardian age'?

5   Thirteen Wasted Years? Some Reflections on Conservative Rule in Britain during the period 1951–64

Superficially, the thirteen years of Conservative rule . . . appear to have been fairly successful ones. Great Britain still behaved as a world power internationally while at home people experienced 'the affluent society' and were told that they had 'never had it so good'. After years of austerity
5   they could afford to relax, and if they spent their money on bingo or beer, who could blame them? Had they not risen to the most supreme of challenges in the World War and had they not, therefore, earned the right to take things easy for a while and to take advantage of the opportunities which Macmillan's hire-purchase society offered them? . . . Everyone
10 from the middle-aged mum with her domestic appliances to teenagers with their transistor radios agreed on that; besides, was there necessarily anything wrong with adopting the lifestyle of the television set or movie screen? The public evidently thought not. . . .
There were, of course, criticisms of the affluent society. Complaints
15 were made about materialistic values, striptease clubs, drink, gambling and the alarming increase in juvenile delinquency, prostitution and illegitimacy. The Profumo and Vassall affairs were held up as examples of a decline in sexual morality and concern was expressed about the waning influence of established religion. But was the Britain of this time really a
20 decadent society in any meaningful sense? Surely not. Young people were certainly more sceptical about traditional values . . . . [but] there is ample evidence to suggest that they cared about cultural values. . . .
    . . . as far as fiscal and economic policy was concerned the Tories did very little in their years of power. Cushioned by the turn in the terms of
25 trade they abolished rationing, reduced taxes and manipulated budgets but they gave little impression of knowing how the economy really worked. Little attention was paid to Britain's sluggish economic growth or the long-term challenge posed by Germany and Japan. Industrial relations were treated with a 'we/they' attitude and no thought was given
30 until late on in the day to the problems created by Britain's prosperity. Instead, the Government sat back and did nothing in the belief that there was nothing to do, and for most of the time their energy was devoted to maintaining Britain as a world power whatever the cost to the economy. . . .

35   Moreover, Tory economic complacency ensured that the necessary economic growth would never be generated. Not enough money was channelled into key industries; stop-go policies undermined the confidence of industry to invest in the long term; too much money was allowed to be exported abroad; and too much money was spent on
40   defence. . . .
        With the economic crises of the early 1960's . . . it began to be apparent that Tory affluence would soon come to an end. The scandals of the Macmillan era merely served to reinforce the impression that a watershed had been reached in the country's history, and foreign affairs
45   seemed to teach a similar lesson. . . . After 1963−4, then, things were never the same again. But in another sense they were never really different.

        A. Sked and C. Cook *Post-War Britain − a Political History*,
        Penguin, 1979, pp. 221−5

Questions

a   (i) What did the slogan 'You never had it so good' mean, and what was its political significance (line 4)?
     (ii) What were the 'years of austerity' (line 4)?
     (iii) What was 'Macmillan's hire-purchase society' (line 9)?
     (iv) What were the 'Profumo and Vassall affairs' (line 17) and what was their political significance?
     (v) What were the 'stop-go policies' (line 37) of the fifties and early sixties?
b   In what ways was it possible to justify the affluent society and why did people accept it so readily?
c   How valid were the criticisms of the affluent society?
d   The Conservative governments failed to understand the structural changes that had occurred in both domestic and international economies. They adopted a policy of complacency. Discuss.
*   e   Are the authors correct in seeing 1963−4 as a watershed?

Further Work

a   To be a historian of contemporary Britain necessitates a full understanding of economics. Discuss.
b   Examine in detail Conservative policy between 1951 and 1964 towards:
     (i) defence;
     (ii) the trade unions;
     (iii) Europe;
     (iv) nationalisation and the public sector;
     (v) taxation.
     In what ways did they change and why?
c   Affluence and consensus were the key concepts of the fifties and early sixties. Both were based on illusion. Is this true?
d   The Campaign for Nuclear Disarmament and the beginnings of rock

music, the 'Angry Young Men' and changing social attitudes were as much a part of this period as Conservative policy. Assess their impact.

e 'Affluent society' or 'Thirteen Wasted Years'. Comment.

f Did the Labour Party offer a clear alternative to Conservative policies between 1951 and 1964?